THE RISE AND DECLINE

OF THE

FREE TRADE MOVEMENT.

THE RISE AND DECLINE

OF THE

FREE TRADE MOVEMENT.

BY

W. CUNNINGHAM, D.D., F.B.A.

HON. FELLOW OF GONVILLE AND CAIUS COLLEGE, FELLOW AND LECTURER
OF TRINITY COLLEGE AND VICAR OF GREAT S. MARY'S, CAMBRIDGE ;
FORMERLY LECTURER ON ECONOMIC HISTORY IN
HARVARD UNIVERSITY.

SECOND EDITION.

CAMBRIDGE:
AT THE UNIVERSITY PRESS.
1905

CAMBRIDGE
UNIVERSITY PRESS

University Printing House, Cambridge CB2 8BS, United Kingdom

Cambridge University Press is part of the University of Cambridge.

It furthers the University's mission by disseminating knowledge in the pursuit of
education, learning and research at the highest international levels of excellence.

www.cambridge.org
Information on this title: www.cambridge.org/9781107433199

© Cambridge University Press 1905

This publication is in copyright. Subject to statutory exception
and to the provisions of relevant collective licensing agreements,
no reproduction of any part may take place without the written
permission of Cambridge University Press.

First published 1905
First paperback edition 2014

A catalogue record for this publication is available from the British Library

ISBN 978-1-107-43319-9 Paperback

Cambridge University Press has no responsibility for the persistence or accuracy of
URLs for external or third-party internet websites referred to in this publication,
and does not guarantee that any content on such websites is, or will remain, accurate
or appropriate.

TO THE

MEMBERS OF THE

COMPATRIOTS CLUB.

The same inventions which make vast political unions possible, tend to make states which are on the old scale of magnitude, unsafe, insignificant, second rate.

SEELEY, *Expansion of England*, 88.

PREFACE.

THIS volume consists of the substance of a course which I gave in the Michaelmas Term of 1903 ; it was planned with the view of presenting to members of the University a dispassionate survey of the main issues involved in the present fiscal controversy. The lectures have been written out from notes which were taken at the time by my daughter, who has also helped me in supplying additional illustrations.

Complaint was made by some of my audience that they could not tell which side I took. I fear I do not know for certain what my views might have been in 1783, or 1823 or 1846 ; I have never speculated about pre-natal political affinities. As to the impending issue, the case is different. It hardly seems possible that any one, who has been influenced by the political ideas of Sir John Seeley and is true to the economic teaching of Adam Smith, should hesitate. I hope to march with the men who have wisdom to reconsider a decision, honesty to acknowledge a blunder, and courage to try to retrieve it.

The demand for a second edition has given me the opportunity of making a few trifling emendations. I have also added to the volume two lectures which have been already published in pamphlet form. *The Real Richard Cobden* was written out from my notes,

and the newspaper reports, of an address I gave on
June 3rd, 1904—the centenary of Cobden's birth—at
a meeting of the Compatriots Club in Cambridge.
Back to Adam Smith is a paper which I read at
Edinburgh on December 15th, 1903, before the
Scottish Society of Economists.

W. C.

TRINITY COLLEGE,
    CAMBRIDGE.
        February 1905.

CONTENTS.

INTRODUCTION.

THE story of the rise and decline of the Free Trade movement has a practical bearing which renders it a matter of general interest at the present time; but it has also a special attraction for students of political phenomena. The agitation may be said to have been unique, for it had its basis in a scientific doctrine. The history of all ages of the world has shewn the play of human aspirations and passions, of racial antipathies and moral ideals; but it was left for the eighteenth century to make a great advance in formulating the knowledge of human society and of the conditions of its prosperity. The Free Trade movement as a political force owed its strength to the fact that it had a scientific character: this seems also to account for its limitations and defects.

The distinctive features may be rendered more clear if we contrast this new type of political force with another element which has at all times played a large part in the history of the world. Religious ideals and aspirations have frequently served to inspire political movements and military conquests. Religious feeling entered deeply into all the conflicts of the pagan world; the advance of Islam, and the efforts of the Crusaders to repel it, were alike affected by religious sentiment. The same sort of feeling was an important factor in the struggles which arose in the eighteenth century about the possession of the East, and the colonisation of the New World. Religion, which is concerned with man's relation to God, has in all ages made itself felt in politics, since it claims to tell men what they *ought* to do, absolutely. But Science makes no such pretension; she is concerned with man's relation to external things. In the eighteenth century Economic Science had at last advanced so far that it was possible for such men as Turgot and Adam Smith to lay down a reasoned statement of the conduct that is *expedient*, with reference to the material prosperity of human beings.

Since their claims are so different, the response which is made to a political appeal will be very different according as it is made in the name of Religion, or on Scientific grounds. When a prophet appears, preaching some action as a duty divinely commanded to be done at all hazards, he works upon the emotions; and his doctrine seems infectious. If once it establishes a hold it may spread with extraordinary rapidity, as the crusading enthusiasm was caught up in so many parts of Christendom. The progress of a scientific principle might be expected to be much more tardy; time is required for the intelligence to be convinced as to the expediency of a new departure. There certainly was no sudden success in the diffusion of Free Trade principles. Pitt, who was entirely convinced of the wisdom of the new economic views, could not carry either the House of Commons or the public with him; but the opinions of Adam Smith gradually obtained a greater hold on the minds of men of education, so that about a quarter of a century after his death they had obtained very general acceptance in the Councils of the Realm.

It might be thought that, just because the scientific principles were built up slowly and accepted with hesitancy, they would hold their own more successfully within their limited sphere. This certainly was the feeling of many economists and publicists at the beginning of last century. The claim of Religion to give absolute guidance in political life appeared to have been hopelessly discredited by the disruption of Christendom, and such struggles as the Wars of the League in France and the Thirty Years' War in Germany, where both sides appealed to the will of the same God. But the reasoned treatment of what was expedient for the material prosperity of the country seemed to leave no room for such uncertainty. Their advocates thought that the new principles rested on a solid basis which could not be shaken. There was more than a trace of superciliousness in the way in which they spoke of less enlightened times. " The reign of Elizabeth though glorious was not one in which sound principles of commerce were known[1]." Elizabethan

---

[1] *Parl. Hist.* xxvii. 564.

practice in restoring the currency, and laying the foundations of English industrial greatness, might perhaps have been studied with advantage at a time when cash payments were suspended, and all attention to technical training was discarded. But these men had no suspicion that the superior wisdom of which they were conscious would ever be called in question. They had no doubt that their principles must obtain increasing acceptance as education spread, and experience gave fresh confirmation. We see that the unexpected has happened; public confidence had been shaken, and it suffered a very serious blow when Gladstone insisted that economic principles were not applicable to the practical problems of Irish life, and might be fitly relegated to Saturn. Nothing has been more curious in the fiscal controversy than the difference of opinion as to the weight which should be attached to the opinion of scientific men dealing with their own subjects[1]. Are we forced either to follow economic authorities blindly, or to repudiate them altogether? Is there no mean between the exaggerated deference which was shewn to the maxims of Political Economy in the middle of last century, and the undue disparagement to which it is exposed in the present day? We must face this question at once, for our whole attitude towards the Free Trade movement must greatly depend on our view as to the reliability of Economic Science as a practical guide in political life.

[1] Compare the excellent article by Prof. J. S. Nicholson, *The Use and Abuse of Authority in Economics* in *Economic Journal*, XIII. 554; also p. 125 below.

The solution of the difficulty is to be found by keeping clearly in mind the necessary limitations of Economic Science: exaggerated expectations on the part of the public have given rise to natural disappointment. Human society is very complex and may be viewed in many aspects for purposes of investigation; Political Economy looks upon it as a mechanism, and considers the play of different factors. It assumes that all persons are actuated by a simple motive—the desire of wealth—and that their actions are in accordance with this dominant force. If we wish to investigate the material condition of society at a particular time, this is the point of view which it is best worth our while to take, so that we may obtain a clear analysis. It is not only convenient but it is sound. A great deal of social action does go on like a mechanism, under the operation of a well-known force, since every man is on the whole struggling for his own interest. But after all, this is not the whole truth; society is a mechanism, but it is not a mere mechanism. If we want either to diagnose the mischiefs from which a community suffers at any time or to suggest remedies, we must not be satisfied to analyse the mechanism of society, but we must study it as an organism with powers of self-adaptation to its environment.

It is easy to find other illustrations of the same sort of inadequacy, and of discussion that is sound so far as it goes, but still very incomplete. For many purposes we can regard the human body as a mechanism; an eight-oared boat is an ingenious and carefully adjusted piece of mechanism. In rowing a race each individual must swing and strike the water with precision; style in rowing is not a mere fashion, but is closely connected with the application of mechanical principles as to the manner in which muscular force can be best applied. But neither a crew, nor any one of the individuals of which it is composed, is a mere machine. The coach has not merely to consider the principles of mechanics, but to be careful that the men are in the best condition; training is an element he must not neglect. When we pass from regarding a crew as a machine to recognise that it consists of several living beings, we enter on an entirely different order of ideas. It would be easy to shew that not only questions of hygiene but of morality may be involved in the composition of an eight; in rowing a severe race there may be risks involved which a man ought not to run, or time he ought not to spare. If we look at the crew as a mechanism we get information that is sound so far as it goes, but is neither final nor complete.

Economics treats society as a mechanism, and it gives us most valuable truth, so far as it goes; but it is never the whole truth. The analysis may be perfectly accurate, but it cannot, from the nature of the case and the point of view adopted, include all the elements that must be taken into account. So far as practical guidance is concerned, we must always bear in mind that the maxims put forward by economists rest on a foundation which is not perfectly secure, but that needs to be tested over and over again.

For our own immediate purpose of mere inquiry and description, this point must also be borne in mind: the varying fortunes of the Free Trade movement have been a most important element in English life for the last century and more. If we are to follow it intelligently in its growth and decline, we must not be content to concentrate our attention on economic phenomena, but we must take account of many affairs which are indirectly and remotely but none the less really connected with the story. It is only in a dead subject that we can sever the nervous from the alimentary system; in the living body they are constantly reacting on one another. Quotations of prices and rates of wages for the last century are dreary reading, if we are content to regard them as illustrations of the operation of supply and demand, and to insist that in each bargain each individual was pursuing his own interest as he conceived it. To understand the changes of social condition and physical opportunity, which made it possible for the man to take from time to time a different view of his interest, is essential to a real grasp of the actual course of affairs: but this must lead us away from the strictly economic aspect to political and social history. We cannot be satisfied with mechanical analogies. We must look at English society as an organism, living and expanding and adapting itself to new conditions all the time, not as a machine, performing the same motions regularly in the same way, though with occasional differences in the speed. It may be necessary and useful, for certain purposes, to regard the economic system of the country at any given time as a machine; but we must take another standpoint if we are to understand the continual adaptation which is going on over long periods in progressive countries. In particular we shall have to notice that sometimes the political affairs of a country —its constitutional and colonial system—are readjusted to meet economic needs, and that at other times the economic system has been adapted to the political environment.

These two sides must certainly be borne in mind if we hope to have any comprehension of the course which has been run by the Free Trade movement. Political views delayed the adoption of a large measure of Free Trade by this country for more than sixty years; economic conditions forced it on and contributed to its success, while political aspirations in other lands have brought about a reaction, and rendered the reconsideration of our attitude inevitable. The point of view of economic science is one it is essential to adopt for the detailed examination of particular episodes, but it is wholly inadequate when we come to survey the course of the movement as a whole.

Economic doctrine is perfectly sound, and very valuable, but it has its limitations. It does not like a religious prophet proclaim an absolute duty; it does not lay down any principle which holds good universally throughout the physical order. It puts forward the means which may be expected under ordinary circumstances to conduce to certain ends, which are very generally desired. The principle of Free Trade declares it is expedient that there should be no restriction on the exchange of goods and services, either between communities or individuals, in order to secure (*a*) the greatest possible mass of goods in the world as a whole, and (*b*) the greatest possibility of immediate comfort for each consumer. That statement appears to me perfectly true, and I do not think it worth while to reiterate the arguments that have been brought forward from the time of Adam Smith and Turgot in order to establish it. We may accept it readily, as a doctrine which no person of intelligence can fail to find convincing; and yet we need not suppose that those who demur to it are necessarily either fools or knaves.

Personally I sympathise entirely and heartily with the objects which the Free Trade advocate assumes : but I can imagine that if I spoke to the first American citizen I might meet on landing in New York, and explained to him that the protective system of the United States was mistaken, because it was inconsistent with the greatest possible production in the world as a whole, he might say that he did not much care about the world as a whole, but that what he wanted was the greatest possible amount of wealth on the spot, in New York. Nor perhaps would he be very much concerned about the comfort of the consumer. The mere consumer appears to be an idle person battening on the labour of other people;

there is much to be said for those who insist that if
there is to be any preference the producers should be
considered primarily. A man may accept the Free
Trade reasoning as perfectly true, but yet feel that
it is entirely unconvincing, because he is not particularly interested in the objects which Free Trade
doctrine takes for granted as lying near the heart of
every right-minded person. To produce the greatest
amount of goods in the world, and to secure for every
consumer the most in the present are objects which
do not appeal to all my friends as much as they
appeal to me. The aim of American protection has
been to build up an independent political community
on the other side of the world; the citizens have been
willing to attempt this at a considerable cost. To
my mind the Free Trade doctrine is economically
sound ; it gives us a basis for examining and estimating the expense at which the protective system
has been carried out ; but it is quite possible for an
American to hold that his game has been worth the
candle. The doctrine that protection is costly to the
consumer may be perfectly sound, and yet it is rightly
disregarded by men who are not content to live
cheaply and comfortably themselves, but are willing
to make some sacrifice in order to attain their
political ideal.

The incompatibility between Free Trade doctrine
and political ambition is inherent in the principles
themselves ; it does not merely arise in connection
with their application to America. As set forward
by Turgot and Adam Smith the doctrine tended to

distract attention from the nation as a political unit, it laid no stress on the well-being of any one country as a centre to which patriotism clings. This tendency to disregard the idea of a nation was probably unconscious. Turgot was inclined to be a theorist, who in the spirit of his age accentuated what was natural, and held good all the world over, as compared with the conventions established in different political communities. Though Adam Smith entitled his book *The Wealth of Nations,* he is chiefly concerned in discussing the wealth of the separate citizens—the conveniences and comforts of the individuals who compose the nations at a given time. The thought of the nation as a unit, and of the gradual development of its resources, is left somewhat in the background. As time went on this tendency became more explicit : in Cobden's eyes one of the advantages of Free Trade was that it made for cosmopolitan influence, and might be expected to weaken the connection between England and her colonies[1]. The question as to the economic prosperity of England under Free Trade is very important, but it is only one side of the matter. We must try to take account of its political conditions and the political influences it has exercised if we are to gauge the character of the movement aright.

[1] Morley, *Life of Cobden,* I. 230.

CHAPTER I.

PITT AND THE REVOLTED COLONIES.

IF we attempted to trace the origin of the Free Trade
movement we should have to go back a long way in
English history. Perhaps we might find the most
convenient starting point in a detailed examination
of the Restoration period, when so much attention
was given to the systematic development of English
industry and commerce. Certainly at that era the
principles of Free Trade were very effectively set
forth by North, Barbon, Davenant, and a group of
Tory pamphleteers[1] who urged that, since the main
benefit of commerce to the country consisted in the
goods that were brought to us for consumption,
intercourse with such a country as France was a
boon. The Whig policy of excluding French goods,
with the view of encouraging the producer and mani-
pulating commercial regulations so that trade might
react favourably on industry, carried the day at the
Revolution, and dominated our English life during

[1] Ashley, *Tory Origin of Free Trade*, in *Surveys*, 268.

the long period when the Whigs controlled the
affairs of State[1]. The seventeenth century pamphleteers had anticipated much of the teaching of
Adam Smith, but they had no real opportunity of
carrying it into effect. The publication of *The
Wealth of Nations* marks the period when the Free
Trade movement came into the sphere of practical
politics. The economic advantages of free intercourse were stated much more fully and convincingly
than had been done by other writers, and the circumstances of our own country were favourable to
attempts to adopt them in more than one direction.
When the issue of the War of Independence rendered
it necessary to place the commerce between England
and America on a new footing, Pitt set himself to
give effect to the new principles, and to introduce
greater facilities for trade, not only with such ports
as New York and Boston, but with France, and with
Ireland as well. The objects he had in view, and
the lengths which he was prepared to go in the
direction of Free Trade, deserve at least a passing
glance. Pitt seems to have been ready to deal with
the economic life of the country without direct
regard to political requirements. The mercantile
system as he found it had been gradually reared by
consciously subordinating every factor of material
prosperity to the object of building up the naval

[1] The Tories failed finally in their attempt to reduce the barriers
which had been erected to prevent trade with France, when Parliament refused to confirm the commercial clauses of the Treaty of
Utrecht in 1713.

power of the country. Pitt seems to have been inclined to break down the main props of the maritime strength of the realm, under the impression that it could stand by its own inherent force, and that the buttresses could be dispensed with. He was prepared to disregard the political considerations which had hitherto been paramount in all the attempts to regulate commercial intercourse between this and other lands.

The fullest expression of his views is to be found in connection with his scheme for the management of Irish affairs. Much of the jealousy of Irish prosperity which had been shewn by the Whig party in Parliament had been due to the fact that the revenue of that country was not under the control of the House of Commons, and that a development of its resources would give the Crown an independent revenue, which would render it possible to disregard constitutional checks on arbitrary power. It was Pitt's first care that a contribution from customs and excise should be made by the Irish Parliament "towards defraying the expense of protecting the general commerce of the Empire in time of peace[1]." He proposed that, on this condition, Irish interests should be no longer treated as subordinate to those of the mother country[2], but that Ireland should be

[1] *Parl. Hist.* xxv. 328.

[2] " There were," he said, "but two possible systems for countries situated in relation to one another like Britian and Ireland. The one, of having the smaller subservient, and subordinate to the greater—to make the one, as it were, an instrument of advantage, and to make all her efforts operate in favour, and conduce merely

"admitted to a permanent and irrevocable participation of the commercial advantages of this country." It was part of his scheme "for the general benefit of the British Empire, that the importation of articles from foreign states should be regulated from time to time in each kingdom, on such terms as may afford an effectual preference to the importation of similar articles of the growth, product and manufacture of the other[1]." He aimed at the wealth and prosperity of the whole Empire and held that the local sources from which they arose might be regarded with indifference[2]. Pitt was prepared to face the

to the interest of, the other. This system we had tried in respect to Ireland. The other was a participation and community of benefits, and a system of equality and fairness, which, without tending to aggrandize the one or depress the other, should seek the aggregate interests of the empire. Such a situation of commercial equality, in which there was to be a community of benefits, demanded also a community of burthens; and it was the situation in which he was anxious to place the two countries." *Parl. Hist.* xxv. 318.

[1] *Parl. Hist.* xxv. 314, Resolution IX.

[2] "The fundamental principle, and the only one on which the whole plan can be justified, is that I mentioned in the beginning of my letter—that for the future the two countries will be to the most essential purposes united. On this ground, the wealth and prosperity of the whole is the object: from what local sources they arise is indifferent. We trust to various circumstances, in believing that no branch of trade or manufacture will shift so suddenly as not to allow time, in every instance as it arises, for the industry of this country gradually to take another direction; and confident that there will be markets sufficient to exercise the industry of both countries, to whatever pitch either can carry it, we are not afraid in this liberal view to encourage a competition which will ultimately prove for the common benefit of the empire, by giving to each country the possession of whatever branch of trade or article of manufacture it is best adapted to, and therefore likely to carry on with the most advantage. These are the ideas I entertain of what

hostility of British manufacturers[1], but he found it impossible to carry through this statesmanlike proposal. Fox played upon English suspicion of Ireland[2]; the English manufacturers, under the leadership of Wedgewood, organised a vigorous agitation in defence of their exclusive privileges, and the sensitiveness of the Irish Parliament to any infraction of its constitutional independence combined with other causes to wreck the measure. Lord Rosebery deplores the manner in which this opportunity of inaugurating a system of Free Trade and preferential tariffs within the Empire was allowed to slip. "When we consider the object and the price: that the price was free trade and the object commercial, and, in all probability, complete union with Ireland;

we give to Ireland, and of the principles on which it is given. The unavoidable consequence of these principles brings me back to that which I set out with—the indispensable necessity of some fixed mode of contribution on the part of Ireland, in proportion to her growing means, to the general defence." *Correspondence between the Right Honourable William Pitt and Charles Duke of Rutland*, 65.

[1] As Pitt writes to the Duke of Rutland, his scheme would give Ireland more than a bare equality with England; but he recognises that if "it were bare equality, we are departing, in order to effect it, from the policy of prohibiting duties so long established in this country. In doing so we are perhaps to encounter the prejudices of our manufacturing [interests] in every corner of the kingdom. We are admitting to this competition a country whose labour is cheap, and whose resources are unexhausted, ourselves burdened with taxes, which are felt in the price of every necessary of life and of course enter into the cost of every article of manufacture." *Ibid.* p. 62.

[2] "The whole tendency of the propositions appeared to him to go the length of appointing Ireland the sole guardian of the laws of navigation, and grand arbitress of all the commercial interests of the Empire." *Parl. Hist.* xxv. 333.

that there was, in fact, no price to pay, but only a double boon, to use Pitt's happy quotation, 'twice blessed; it blesseth him that gives and him that takes,' it is difficult to avoid the impression that there has been throughout the past history of England and Ireland a malignant fate counteracting every auspicious chance, and blighting each opportunity of beneficence as it arises[1]."

Pitt's action in regard to France is less instructive so far as his policy is concerned : but it was not so futile as his Irish scheme. He had at least a temporary success in opening up a larger measure of free intercourse with France, by the treaty which was concluded in 1786. He had to meet the fierce opposition of Fox, who "contended that France was the natural foe of Great Britain and wished by entering into a commercial treaty with us to tie our hands," but Pitt defended the agreement most ably on fiscal[2] and political grounds. "By promoting habits of friendly intercourse, and of mutual benefit, while it invigorated the resources of Britain it made it less likely that she should have occasion to call

[1] Lord Rosebery, *Pitt*, 75.

[2] "The surrender of revenue for great commercial purposes was a policy by no means unknown in the history of Great Britain; but here we enjoyed the extraordinary advantage of having it returned to us in a three-fold rate, by extending and legalizing the importation of the articles. When it was considered that the increase must exceed the concession which we made it would no longer be an argument that we cannot afford this reduction. Increase by means of reduction, he was obliged to confess, appeared once a paradox; but experience had now convinced us that it was more than practicable." *Parl. Hist.* xxvi. 389.

forth these resources. It certainly had at least the
happy tendency to make the two nations enter into
more intimate communion with one another, to enter
into the same views even of taste and manners: and
while they were mutually benefited by the connection,
and endeared to one another by the result of the
common benefits, it gave a better chance for the
preservation of harmony between them, while, so far
from weakening, it strengthened their sinews for
war[1]." Pitt's anticipations were not realised: the
treaty was not popular in England, but in France
the opposition gathered in strength as time went on.
English manufacturers were so far successful in
flooding the French markets with goods that the
native producers demanded a return to a protective
policy. There was a revulsion from the Free Trade
principles of Turgot and his associates under the
Revolutionary government, and the agreement came
to an end.

The United States of America were much more
willing than any other power to respond to Pitt's
proposals for increased freedom of intercourse. Turgot
had himself recognised that the ideas he had done
so much to disseminate would find a congenial soil
on the other side of the Atlantic. Some[2] months
before the American colonies had actually declared
their independence, he drew up a *Memoir*[3] in which

[1] *Parl. Hist.* xxvi. 392.

[2] This and the following paragraphs have already appeared in
the *Economic Review* for Jan. 1904.

[3] *Memoir*, dated 6 April, 1776, in *Œuvres*, viii. 434.

he stated his grounds for thinking that the colonists
would be successful, and gave a forecast of the
economic policy they would probably pursue. "It
will be a wise and happy thing for the Nation which
shall be the first to modify its policy according to the
new conditions, and to be content to regard its
colonies as if they were allied provinces and not
subjects of the mother country. It will be a wise
and happy thing for the Nation which is the first to
be convinced that the secret of success, so far as
commercial policy is concerned, consists in employing
all its land in the manner most profitable for the
proprietory, all the hands in the manner most advantageous to the workmen personally, that is to say
in the manner in which each would employ them if
we would let him be simply directed by his own
interest, and that all the rest of mercantile policy is
vanity and vexation of spirit. When the entire
separation of America shall have forced the whole
world to recognise this truth and purged the European
nations of commercial jealousy, there will be one
great cause of war the less in the world." And when
the colonies had been successful in the field, and
during the critical period when the separate states
were feeling their way towards a settled Constitution,
there were leading statesmen in America who would
have been glad to see their country play the part
which Turgot had anticipated, and set an example to
the world of the benefits of Free Trade. Jefferson,
who was much influenced by French writers, spoke
decidedly on the subject. "I think," he wrote to

John Adams in 1785, "all the world would gain by setting commerce at perfect liberty." He regarded the "natural" progress of opulence, and the development of the United States as a nation of farmers, to be the wisest course for his countrymen to pursue. "We have now," he says, "lands enough to employ an infinite number of people in their cultivation. Cultivators of the earth are the most valuable citizens. They are the most vigorous, the most independent, the most virtuous, and they are tied to their country, and wedded to its liberty and interests by the most lasting bonds. As long, therefore, as they can find employment in this line, I would not convert them into mariners, artisans, or anything else. But our citizens will find employment in this line till their numbers and of course their productions become too great for the demand, both internal and foreign. This is not the case as yet, and probably will not be for a considerable time. As soon as it is, the surplus of hands must be turned to something else; I should then, perhaps, wish to turn them to the sea, in preference to manufacturers, because comparing the characters of the two classes, I find the former the most valuable citizens. " I consider," he goes on, "the class of artificers as panders of vice, and the instruments by which the liberties of a country are generally overturned[1]." At this date,

---

[1] Tucker, *Life of Thomas Jefferson*, I. 200; also more fully in *Notes on Virginia*, 275. At a later date he admitted that he had been mistaken. He modestly accepted Austin's suggestion that the purity of his mind had rendered it impossible for him to

then, the Free Trade course seemed to him to be preferable, both on economic and political grounds; and Alexander Hamilton, whose social connections were entirely different, since he desired to render the capitalist and commercial classes[1] dominant in the new nation, was ready to admit the soundness of Free Trade principles. In the *Memoir* on manufactures which he wrote in 1791, he summarises Turgot's doctrine, and adds that if it had governed the conduct of nations more generally than it has

conceive the depravity of European statesmen (*The soundness of the policy of protecting domestic manufactures*, 1817, p. 8). "Who in 1785 could foresee the rapid depravity which was to render the close of that century a disgrace to the history of man? Who could have imagined that the two most distinguished in the rank of nations, for science and civilisation, would have suddenly descended from that honourable eminence, and, setting aside all those moral laws established by the Author of Nature between nation and nation, as between man and man, would cover earth and sea with robberies and piracies, merely because strong enough to do it with temporal impunity, and that under this disbandment of nations from social order we should have been despoiled of a thousand ships, and have thousands of our artisans reduced to Algerian slavery. Yet all this has taken place. The British interdicted to our vessels all harbours of the globe, without having first proceeded to some one of hers, these paid a tribute proportioned to the cargo, and obtained her license to proceed to the port of destination. The French declared them to be lawful prize if they had touched at the port, or been visited by a ship of the enemy nation. Thus we were completely excluded from the ocean....We have experienced what we did not then believe, that there exist both profligacy and power enough to exclude us from the field of interchange with other nations. That to be independent for the comforts of life we must fabricate them ourselves....Experience has now taught me that manufactures are now as necessary to our independence as to our comfort." Randolf, *Memoirs*, IV. 278.

[1] Rabbeno, *American Commercial Policy*, 293, 300.

done, "there is room to suppose that it might have carried them faster to prosperity and greatness[1]."

When we find the author of the *Declaration of Independence* and the virtual framer of the *Constitution* agreed in accepting these principles, when we remember the extraordinary difficulty which was found in creating an authority that should be capable of devising and enforcing an economic policy for the whole country, we cannot but be surprised that America did not develop as a Free Trade country from the first. The reason was very simple; American statesmen did not feel free to apply their principles[2]; they were forced into legislative efforts to foster

[1] *Report on Manufactures* (1793), p. 4.

[2] Hamilton puts the matter as follows:—" If the system of perfect liberty to industry and commerce were the prevailing system of nations, the argument which dissuades a country, in the predicament of the United States, from the zealous pursuit of manufactures would doubtless have great force....But the system which has been mentioned is far from characterising the general policy of nations. The prevalent one has been regulated by an opposite spirit. The consequence is that the United States are to a certain extent precluded from foreign commerce. They can indeed, without difficulty, obtain from abroad the manufactured supplies of which they are in want, but they experience numerous and very injurious impediments to the omission and vent of their own commodities....A constant and increasing necessity on their part, for the commodities of Europe, and only a partial and occasional demand for their own in return, could not but expose them to a state of impoverishment compared with the opulence to which their political and natural advantages authorise them to aspire...." He adds, " If Europe will not take from us the products of our soil on terms consistent with our interest, the natural remedy is to contract as far as possible our wants of her." Hamilton, *Report of the Secretary of the Treasury of the United States on the Subject of Manufactures*, p. 31.

shipping and manufactures in self-defence, and as
a consequence of the action of other countries, and
especially of England.

Pitt was convinced that it was to the interest of
England to develop her trade with North America to
the fullest extent, and realised that this could be
most certainly done by permitting maritime inter-
course to continue on the same conditions on which
it was carried on while Massachusetts and the other
States had still been parts of the British Empire.
He was ready to waive the policy of the Navigation
Acts, and to allow American ships to ply between the
English West Indian Islands and New England.
But English shipowners were unwilling to relinquish
any part of their monopoly of the carrying trade.
Lord Sheffield made himself their spokesman in his
Observations on the Commerce of the American States.
Pitt was clear that our wisest course was to open an
intercourse with America as early as possible in order
to prevent other countries from getting the start of
us and carrying their goods to the American market[1].
He hoped by conceding to their shipowners a footing
in the West Indian trade to secure the maintenance
of a practical monopoly of the American demand for
manufactures. When Fox came into power the
policy prevailed of maintaining the Navigation Acts,
and this was tantamount to new restrictions. The
measures he proposed were quite inadequate from the
point of view of those who desired to preserve the

---

[1] *Parl. Hist.* XXIII. 725.

prosperity of the West Indian Islands[1]. But the ultimate influence on the American States was far more serious: the New Englanders were compelled in self-defence to enter into commercial and industrial rivalry with Great Britian. They soon found as a matter of fact that economic independence was essential if their political independence was to be

[1] " The Petitioner has received Accounts from Jamaica, since the Publication thereof, that the above Order has already operated most grievously to the People of that Island; that Lumber, and other American Commodities, rose at once to nearly the War Price, and that it was particularly hard on the Inhabitants of Kingston, who had begun to rebuild the Houses burnt about two Years ago; and that this Order is deemed equal to a Prohibition, as it is not probable that the Americans will admit British Ships into their Ports, whilst they are precluded from ours; and representing to the House, that the Planters in general in the said Island, being deeply involved in Debt, and taxed both in Great Britain and in Jamaica beyond what their Produce will bear, instead of being loaded with new Oppressions, require every Assistance and Indulgence that can possibly be held out to them, but more particularly in the Articles of Lumber and Provisions, as their very Existence depends upon the Reduction of those necessary Expenses of their Estates; and that the Petitioner sees the Propriety and Necessity of Great Britain's Attention to the Carrying Trade and her keeping as much of it as she possibly can to herself, but he sees at the same Time the Impracticability of excluding the Americans from it in the West Indian Islands, as they will carry their Lumber and Provisions to the French, Dutch, Danish, and other Islands, not under the Dominion of His Majesty, to the singular and partial Emoluments of those Islands, from whence they will be clandestinely carried to our Islands, loaded with double Freight, double Port Charges, double loading and unloading, Charges of going through a Second Hand, and the Provisions in particular in a worse and unwholesome Condition : And therefore praying, That so much of the said Act as empowers His Majesty in Council to issue Orders and Directions, as in the said act mentioned, may not be continued, or if continued, may be limited and restricted in such Manner, that the Island of Jamaica may receive no further Detriment thereby." *Commons Journals*, xxxix. p. 840.

a reality. They were crowded out of a lucrative trade, while a few years later, in the time of the French Revolution and of the Continental System, the Americans were seriously distressed because of the interruption of the usual supplies of foreign manufactures. What they desired was room to grow, freedom to allow of healthy and natural economic development, and this they could not get without taking pains to foster a mercantile marine and to protect manufactures. The opponents of Pitt converted the United States to the impracticability of being Pioneers in a Free Trade movement, and they were not deterred from fostering manufactures by the solemn warning of an English Economic expert[1] as to the absurdity of their attempt.

Thus it happened that all the experiments which Pitt had endeavoured to make in Free Trade were frustrated. There can be no doubt that his views were economically sound ; but when we view the matter in its political aspect it is hardly possible in retrospect to condemn the somewhat narrow patriotism of Fox and his associates ; in the disturbed state of the world, Pitt's scheme was premature[2]. England had emerged from one great struggle, but she was about to enter on another that would try her resources more severely ; there was no guarantee of continued peace in the world at large. The contest

[1] *On Manufactures in America*, 1797, in *Annals of Agriculture*, xxix. 131.

[2] There is also room for doubt whether it would have been really favourable to the constitutional development of the colonies. See below, p. 153.

with Napoleon turned on the possession of dominant power by sea : it is probable that if the Navigation Act had been relaxed and American shipping had developed earlier, the difficulty in regard to neutral trading would have been greater, and it is possible that the issue might not have been the same. Such speculations may be idle, but at least we may feel that the final struggle with France was not one in which England could afford to forego any advantage.

CHAPTER II.

HUSKISSON AND TARIFF REFORM.

i. *Thorough-going protection.*

A GENERATION elapsed from the time when Pitt carried through his French treaty in 1786 before any further step was taken in the direction of breaking down the complicated restrictions and limitations which had been imposed, with the view of regulating our trade to the greatest advantage. The methods of fostering economic life which had been carefully thought out in the days of Lord Burleigh, were put into effect systematically by Walpole, and carried on with great success during the eighteenth century. The building up of the maritime power of the country was the great object in mind; the development of fisheries and of the mercantile marine were means on which reliance was placed with the view of attaining this end.

Though encouragements to shipping were placed in the forefront in the Elizabethan Age, they were never an exclusive object of attention. Under all the Stuarts, and more particularly after the Restoration, great pains were taken to improve manufactures, and especially to regulate commerce in such a fashion that it should react favourably on industrial development. Spain had created a great maritime and colonial power, but she afforded a warning rather than an example to Englishmen. They had already realised, at the time of the Armada, that her strength was not overwhelming; it appeared that the expansion of mining enterprise in the colonies had been almost injurious, from the way in which it caused a drain on resources at home. Englishmen were nervously anxious to avoid this blunder, and to develop their commerce, together with the consequent colonial expansion, on lines in which it should stimulate and foster native industrial energy. In this they followed the Industrial System which is associated with the name of Colbert in France, and they tried to organise trade so that it should bring raw materials to our shores, and should also "afford a vent" for our finished goods in lands across the sea.

The regulation of commerce, so as to foster industry, was, as it were, the second plank in the Mercantile System; a third was added in the period succeeding the Revolution. Once more Spain could be viewed as a warning, while Holland gave an example to be followed. Agriculture did not flourish in Spain; her dependence on an imported food-supply was a source of weakness, and the Dutch did a profitable business in transporting corn from the Baltic to the Iberian peninsula. The Corn Bounty Act of 1689

was intended to stimulate English agricultural production so as to provide an adequate food supply for
home consumption even in unfavourable seasons;
while at the same time in good years there was an
ample surplus, which our ships could be profitably
employed in exporting. It thus came about that the
Mercantile System in its final form, as it was maintained in the eighteenth century, was by no means so
one-sided as its name implies, but was an all-round
system. It took account of the interaction of the
several interests, and aimed at the complete development of all the economic resources of the country, so
as to give a firm basis to her political power.

So far as its political objects were concerned, the
Mercantile System had proved its success when
Napoleon was forced to succumb in 1815. The
power of England had increased in an extraordinary
fashion, during the period when this scheme of
economic policy was in vogue; and it certainly
seems as if the means employed had been well
adapted to the end in view. It is scarcely possible
for us to realise to what a low position England had
sunk at the time when Burleigh began to guide her
destinies. Elizabeth was utterly destitute of the
means of defending the realm at the outset of her
reign. There was no plant for casting guns, and no
workmen who were competent to do it. For supplies
of ammunition we were dependent on foreign powers;
sulphur and other ingredients for the manufacture of
gunpowder were principally brought from countries
under papal influence. England was utterly un-

prepared for a quarrel with Spain, at the time when
the reign of Philip and Mary came to an end, and
a rupture seemed to be imminent. Good use was
made, however, of the interval which elapsed before
the Invincible Armada actually sailed. Works had
been started, and skilled artisans brought from
abroad, so that the English ordnance was superior to
that of Spain. This was the turning point; and the
general scheme of policy, which had been so successful
under Burleigh's care, was pursued with similar results
through all the constitutional changes of the seventeenth century. English resources increased and the
power of the realm developed; the country was
able to take a foremost place in the eighteenth
century, and to hold her own against Napoleon's
desperate efforts to destroy her. Despite the burden
of taxation, the strain on her credit, and the deprecia-
tion of her money, she had an enormous marine, and
was well able to fit and victual her ships. She could
command foreign markets and her industry increased
by leaps and bounds, even while the strain of the
war was most severe. It is difficult to conceive of
any more startling development of political greatness,
than that which took place under the Mercantile
System.

This growth in political influence and naval
strength may be said to have been almost entirely
due to the increase of material wealth, from which
the sinews of war could be drawn. We have no
means of accurately gauging the extraordinarily
rapid progress which took place in every department

of economic life under this highly protective system, but the broad conclusion is unimpeachable. There is ample evidence that an advance had been made in every sort of manufactures between the reign of Charles II. and 1786. At the former period the English complained that they were ruined by the fine goods imported from France; when intercourse was reopened by Pitt, the French manufacturers could not hold their own against English competition. This was only the beginning of the change; the improved implements introduced by Kaye and Hargreaves were coming into general use, but there had been very little application of power in the textile trades. Success had been attained in the use of coal for smelting and manufacturing iron, and the enormous . development of the hardware and engineering trades was just commencing. Enterprise was also being shewn in the development of coal mining and the improved facilities for internal communication. The steady development and sudden expansion of industrial activity, which rendered England the workshop of the world, occurred under a highly protective system.

The progress of agriculture had also been remarkable; the relative stagnation of centuries came to an end, and the eighteenth century was the era of spirited proprietors, who devoted themselves sedulously and at considerable cost to the introduction of better husbandry. Tull introduced a revolution in the cultivation of roots, and Bakewell was a pioneer in the scientific breeding of stock. We can hardly

suppose that it was a mere accident that the period
when the Corn Bounty policy was in force should
have been marked by the discarding of traditional
methods, and the development of unwonted enterprise
in the management of land[1].

That a period of high protection should have been
characterised by great enterprise and rapid progress
is so entirely inconsistent with the preconceived
opinions of some economists that they are tempted
either to ignore the fact as mere "ancient history,"
or to attempt to explain it away[2]. It is often asserted,
as an axiomatic truth, that protection is enervating,
and that the bracing air of competition is necessary
to stimulate progress. That protection may sometimes lull men into being content with slovenly or
inefficient methods is highly probable, but I cannot
believe that this is always the case; it seems
to me to be largely a matter of personal qualities,
whether a bracing air invigorates or benumbs. Protection affords the protected persons an opportunity
of gain in their callings. If a man is enterprising he
will be inclined to make the most of this opportunity;
if he is sluggish, he may consider that the gain that

[1] Another great era of agricultural improvement began in 1836,
while a protective policy was in force. R. E. Prothero, in *Social
England*, vi. 212.

[2] The report of the committee on agricultural distress in 1821
urges that the great period of improvement took place after 1773,
when the protection for English corn growers was reduced. They
did not apparently take into account that in 1773 the new methods
of agricultural improvement had passed out of the experimental
stage, and that less encouragement was needed to induce men to
adopt what was already a proved success.

is secured to him is good enough and not be at pains
to increase it. We might even distinguish between
the two factors in the production of wealth—labour
and capital. There is generally an element of com-
pulsion and discipline in getting a full day's work out
of the labourer; it is true that necessity is to some
extent a stimulating influence; and possibly, as has
been alleged, the best way to ensure that land should
be well worked by cottiers or small farmers was to
"salt it well with rent." Pressure of some kind is
quite likely to elicit more strenuous effort.

But with capital, especially with the sinking of
capital in a new undertaking, the case is different.
Capital goes where it is attracted, not where it is
compelled. Unless there is some probability that the
outlay will be replaced at a profit, capital will not be
invested in new machines or expensive plant. A low
rate of interest, with no appreciable risk and no worry,
can always be obtained for it. Chronic insecurity
and the danger of being exposed to competition with
subsidised rivals do not seem to me to be obviously
the most favourable conditions for the development of
industry, in an age when capital has become the
dominating influence in production. However that
may be, the fact remains that the eighteenth century,
when protection was carried out most consistently,
was a period of wholly unique progress both in
agricultural and industrial enterprise.

ii.　*The necessity of a change.*

There was, however, another side; in spite of its
real success, both political and economical, the Mercantile System was condemned in 1820 as very
unsatisfactory; it was from many points of view
unwholesome, and it was certainly out of date.

During the seventeenth century the land of the
country had been the great fund from which the
revenue was principally drawn; it had been politically
desirable to render the conditions of life as favourable
as possible to the agricultural classes, since they bore
the main share of the public burdens. But farther,
since the landed men bore the chief burden, it was
not unnatural that they should enjoy a very large
share of political power. The great mercantile
interests were not adequately represented, and the
manufacturing classes were hardly enfranchised at
all, before the reform of 1832. In the course of the
eighteenth and early nineteenth centuries the rapid
development of the trading and industrial classes had
entirely altered their importance relatively to the
landed interest in the community; but the constitutional system of the country had not been brought
into accord with the economic change. In the
counties, and still more in the close burghs, the
landed gentry were able to exercise the influence
of a privileged class; and the effort to bolster up
these privileges had given rise to wide-spread administrative inefficiency and political corruption. The

evil had been aggravated by the Corn Law of 1815, which helped to maintain the status and prosperity of the landed proprietors at the expense of the community generally[1]. It was most important that some steps should be taken which should bring the welfare of the community as a whole into clearer light, and give a far larger body of citizens an effective voice in the government of the country. The power of the landed gentry was a survival from a state of society which England had outgrown, and Cobden had a genuine enthusiasm for breaking it down, and for cutting away any props that supported it.

The system was out of date, not merely politically but commercially; it had taken shape while medieval ideas were still dominant in the management of trade, and it had never been thoroughly adapted to the modern conditions which had come into vogue during the eighteenth century. The medieval merchant was not a mere private person, but a public character with special status and responsibilities: a private individual could not obtain a footing in a foreign town so as to transact business regularly; it was only through belonging to an authorised company that he was able to carry on his trade. As a consequence he was bound to consider, not merely his own private advantage but the policy of the company in the manner in which he did business, and to conform his practice to the rules of "well-ordered trade," which were supposed to take account not of the immediate benefit of individuals but of the continual prosperity

[1] See p. 56 below.

3—2

of the trading interest. The medieval merchant shipped a stock of goods and tried to sell them at the highest price he could; the regulations of his company were intended to prevent any risk of his failing to get a fair profit on each transaction; he had very little idea of stimulating a demand by offering his goods at a low price, and thus disposing of a large quantity on remunerative terms. The company system, whatever its merits may have been, left little scope for initiative; and in the seventeenth century the "straggling merchants" and "interlopers" made strenuous efforts to break down this well-ordered trade; during the eighteenth century they were successful in obtaining the right to engage in almost every branch of trade. They thus broke down the rules of the companies, and left each trader free to carry on his business in the manner which he regarded as most profitable. So soon as the right of the individual trader, as against the company, was thus recognised, the question came to be raised as to the expediency of all the regulations laid down by the State in the supposed interest of trade. Why should the State interfere with the bargains which any man chose to drive, except in so far as it was necessary to raise revenue? Why should not every merchant be left as free as possible to transport what he liked, where he liked, in any ship which was available? A mass of rules of considerable antiquity and doubtful utility survived till 1825 in regard to the industry of the realm. It had ceased to be clear why government should make any regulations for the good of the trade of the country. They seemed to be inexpedient since they hampered individual enterprise, and in the new conditions of trade,—when intercourse was more frequent, and the facilities of credit and new developments of industry made it possible to meet any new demand by an increased supply,—the whole atmosphere of commercial life was inconsistent with the maintenance of the highly organised mercantile system which had proved so beneficial in earlier days.

Society is so complex that the judgment, as to the success or failure of any particular line of policy, will often depend on the criterion we apply. The parliamentary Colbertism of the eighteenth century had been successful in raising the maritime strength of the country to an unprecedented height: but the result on the welfare of the community, in the earlier part of the nineteenth century, was deplorable. The condition of the labouring classes, both in town and country, was miserable in the extreme. The introduction of machinery had caused an enormous expansion of industry on the whole; but it had taken place in a series of violent fluctuations. The periods of good trade had given the enterprising employer the opportunity of piling up a large fortune, but there had also been times when business was carried on at a loss; the position of the wage earners was severely depressed, and many of the skilled operatives in the cotton trade were habitually dependent on assistance from the rates[1]. The rural districts were

[1] Compare in regard to Oldham, *Reports*, 1824, vi. 405, with 1834, xxviii. 921.

in an even worse condition; they had been denuded
of remunerative opportunities of domestic employment, the labourers of many districts had been
reduced to a miserable state of hopeless degradation[1],
while the capital of innumerable tenant farmers had
been exhausted in a desperate struggle for existence.
In addition there was a great difficulty about the
finances of the realm; the pressure of taxation was
very severe, and it was difficult for the administration
to pay its way, or to do anything to reduce the
enormous burden of debt. However they might
differ in diagnosing the nature of the malady, all
public-spirited men were agreed that the economic
condition of the country was very serious, and that
it was necessary to devise some kind of remedy.

iii.   *The adaptation of the revenue system to modern commercial conditions.*

Huskisson has the credit of determining the
manner in which it was wise to deal with the difficulties of the situation. He realised that commerce had come to be the main factor in English
prosperity, and he was inclined both by tradition and
education[2] to favour the principle of rendering commercial intercourse as free as possible[3]. The landed

---

[1] Wakefield, *Swing unmasked* (1831), p. 9.

[2] As a young man he had resided in Paris and come in contact
with the circle of economists there. *Biographical Memoir* in
Speeches, i. 9.

[3] "An open trade, especially to a rich and thriving country, is
infinitely more valuable than any monopoly." *Speeches*, ii. 321.

interest did not now occupy even the second rank; there had been centuries when English trade consisted chiefly in exporting such raw products as wool or corn, and when the progress of commerce was closely connected with the development of rural resources. In the nineteenth century these interests were almost antagonistic; the shippers depended on the manufacturers for their exports, and products such as corn were the most convenient returns they could import. The economic life of the country could best be developed on lines that were quite different from those which had seemed most desirable at the beginning of the eighteenth century; and what had formerly been helps had become hindrances. The restrictions which fettered English trade were of two distinct kinds ; on the one hand there were definite regulations as to the ships which might be employed and the points between which commerce should be carried on by Englishmen, while on the other the customs-tariff had been drawn up, not so much with regard to the revenue, as with a view of favouring national development on healthy lines. Huskisson was concerned in reducing the malign influence exerted on commerce by existing restrictions of all kinds, but his most lasting work was in the changes which were begun in connection with the revenue system of the country.

The demands of the commercial community had been formulated by Thomas Tooke in the Merchants' Petition of 1820—

"That foreign commerce is eminently conducive

to the wealth and prosperity of the country, by
enabling it to import the commodities for the production of which the soil, climate, capital and industry
of other countries are best calculated, and to export
in payment those articles for which its own situation
is better adapted; that freedom from restraint is
calculated to give the utmost extension to foreign
trade, and the best direction to the capital and
industry of the country; that the maxim of buying
in the cheapest market and selling in the dearest,
which regulates every merchant in his individual
dealings, is strictly applicable as the best rule for the
trade of the whole nation; that a policy founded on
these principles would render the commerce of the
world an interchange of mutual advantages, and
diffuse an increase of wealth and enjoyments among
the inhabitants of each state; that, unfortunately,
a policy, the very reverse of this, has been, and is
more or less adopted and acted upon by the government of this and of every other country; each trying
to exclude the productions of other countries, with
the specious and well-meant design of encouraging
its own productions; thus inflicting on the bulk of
its subjects, who are consumers, the necessity of
submitting to privations in the quantity or quality of
commodities, and thus rendering what ought to be
the source of mutual benefit and of harmony among
states, a constantly recurring occasion of jealousy
and hostility; that the prevailing prejudices in favour
of the protective or restrictive system may be traced
to the erroneous supposition that every importation

of foreign commodities occasions a diminution or
discouragement of our own productions to the same
extent; whereas, it may be clearly shown, that
although the particular description of production
which could not stand against unrestrained foreign
competition would be discouraged; yet, as no importation could be continued for any length of time
without a corresponding exportation, direct or indirect,
there would be an encouragement for the purpose of
that exportation of some other production to which
our situation might be better suited ; thus affording
at least an equal, and probably a greater, and certainly
a more beneficial employment to our capital and
labour; that of the numerous protective and prohibitory duties of our commercial code, it may be proved,
that while all operate as a very heavy tax on the
community at large, very few are of any ultimate
benefit to the classes in whose favour they were
originally instituted, and none to the extent of the
loss occasioned by them to other classes; that among
the other evils of the restrictive or protective system,
not the least is, that the artificial protection of one
branch of industry, or source of production against
foreign competition is set up as a ground of claim by
other branches for similar protection; so that if the
reasoning upon which these restrictive or prohibitory
regulations are founded were followed out consistently,
it would not stop short of excluding us from all
foreign commerce whatsoever; and the same train of
argument, which with corresponding prohibitions and
protective duties should exclude us from foreign

trade, might be brought forward to justify the re-
enactment of restrictions upon the interchange of
productions (unconnected with public revenue) among
the kingdoms composing the union, or among the
counties of the same kingdom; that an investigation
of the effects of the restrictive system at this time is
peculiarly called for, as it may, in the opinion of the
petitioners, lead to a strong presumption that the
distress which now so generally prevails, is considerably aggravated by that system; and that some
relief may be obtained by the earliest practicable removal of such of the restraints as may be shewn to
be most injurious to the capital and industry of the
community, and to be attended with no compensating
benefit to the public revenue; that a declaration
against the anti-commercial principles of our restrictive system is of the more importance at the present
juncture, inasmuch as in several instances of recent
occurrence the merchants and manufacturers in
foreign states have assailed their respective governments with applications for further protective or
prohibitory duties and regulations, urging the example
and authority of this country, against which they are
almost exclusively directed, as a sanction for the
policy of such measures; and certainly, if the reasoning upon which our restrictions have been defended
is worth anything, it will apply in behalf of the
regulations of foreign states against us; they insist
upon our superiority in capital and machinery, as we
do upon their comparative exemption from taxation,
and with equal foundation; that nothing would more

tend to counteract the commercial hostility of foreign
states than the adoption of a more enlightened and
more conciliatory policy on the part of this country;
that although as a matter of mere diplomacy it may
sometimes answer to hold out the removal of particular prohibitions or high duties, as depending upon
corresponding concessions by other states in our
favour, it does not follow that we should maintain
our restrictions in cases where the desired concessions
on their part cannot be obtained; our restrictions
would not be the less prejudicial to our own capital
and industry, because the governments persisted in
preserving impolitic regulations; that, upon the
whole, the most liberal would prove to be the most
politic course on such occasions; that, independent
of the direct benefit to be derived by this country on
every occasion of such concession or relaxation, a
great incidental object would be gained by the
recognition of a sound principle or standard to which
all subsequent arrangements might be referred, and
by the salutary influence which a promulgation of
such just views, by the legislature and by the nation
at large, could not fail to have on the policy of other
states; that in thus declaring, as the petitioners do,
their conviction of the impolicy and injustice of the
restrictive system, and in desiring every practicable
relaxation of it, they have in view only such parts of
it as are not connected, or are only subordinately so,
with the public revenue; as long as the necessity for
the present amount of revenue subsists the petitioners
cannot expect so important a branch of it as the

customs to be given up, nor to be materially
diminished, unless some substitute less objectionable
be suggested, but it is against every restrictive regulation of trade not essential to the revenue, against all
duties merely protective from foreign competition,
and against the excess of such duties as are partly
for the purpose of revenue and partly for that of
protection, that the prayer of the present petition is
respectfully submitted to the wisdom of Parliament;
the petitioners therefore humbly pray that the House
will be pleased to take the subject into consideration,
and to adopt such measures as may be calculated to
give greater freedom to foreign commerce, and thereby to increase the resources of the State[1]."

The petitioners were so confident in the strength
of the industrial position of England that they were
quite decided in approving of insular Free Trade, and
insisted that the abolition of all restriction must be to
the benefit of this country.   In 1820 English industry
occupied a unique position; business men could
cherish the confident expectation that they would be
able to "dump" English manufactures on every
other part of the globe for all time.   They had no
hesitation in recommending that Great Britain should
adopt a thorough-going policy of Free Intercourse,
without any regard to the practice of our neighbours.
We had a monopoly of mechanical production.
Apart from our natural advantages in the possession
of coal and iron, there was no immediate prospect

[1] May 8, 1820. *Parliamentary Debates*, N.S. i. 179. Tooke,
History of Prices, vi. 332.

that this monopoly would be broken down as legislative enactments prohibited the export of machines and the emigration of the artisans who had the skill to make, to repair, or to use them. The one thing that seemed necessary for the unlimited development of English trade and industry was that hindrances should be removed, so that we might be able to crush rival industries in every part of the world, by supplying the markets with goods produced on the better and cheaper methods which were only practised in England. Even under these circumstances, however, the government were averse to adopting Free Trade principles absolutely; Huskisson only consented to grant as much practical relaxation as was consistent with retaining the principle of the old system, and maintaining the duty of the State to regulate trade so as to promote the maritime power and industrial prosperity of the country. Huskisson recognised that under changed conditions these objects must be pursued in a new way; but he did not feel free to admit the contention that the statesman should confine his attention to politics, and cease to attempt to foster the economic life of the country. He took tentative measures for increasing freedom of intercourse, and he had no scruple in setting aside existing interests when they seemed to be obstacles to further progress. He pursued the old objects on much more liberal economic principles than his predecessors had done, but he never admitted that he had abandoned the traditional system. He was willing to depart from it, in so far as other nations would do the like.

He was fully persuaded that reciprocity with other nations in shipping facilities "would lead to an increase of the commercial advantages of the country; and while at the same time it had a direct tendency to promote and establish a better political feeling, and to increase confidence among the maritime Powers, it would abate the sources of that commercial jealousy, idly wasting their force in a race of mutual annoyance. It was high time, in the improved state of the civilisation of the world, to establish more liberal principles, and to shew that commerce was not the end, but the means of diffusing comfort and enjoyment among the nations embarked in its pursuit[1]."

The practical relaxations which he made in regard to the employment of foreign shipping were very considerable. Hitherto a decided preference had been shewn to British shipowners, as heavier customs duties were charged on goods imported in vessels sailing under the flags of foreign countries. Other nations were copying the prohibitions by which we had built up our mercantile marine. It was becoming necessary in some trades to have two sets of ships employed[2],—"to have British ships to bring home American produce, and American ships to convey our produce to that country." This absurd state of affairs could only be got rid of by admitting other Powers to a "perfect equality and reciprocity of shipping duties. But this reciprocity with foreigners was quite consistent with the granting of preferences to our own colonies, and with the practice of imposing

[1] Huskisson, *Speeches*, II. 205. [2] *Ib.* II. 204.

penalties on those countries which would not meet our advances[1]." Huskisson was successful in obtaining powers to abolish the discriminating duties in the case of any country which would treat our ships with equal favour. Before six years had expired all the important commercial countries had agreed to this arrangement; and freedom of shipping was established between England and all foreign lands, while colonial trade was opened to any country which reciprocated by allowing us to trade with her colonies. The preference which was retained for British shipping lay in the fact that foreign vessels were excluded from taking part in the coasting trade, and this was defined as including all intercommunication between the mother country and the colonies. This restriction continued, and became an element of discord at a later time[2], but there was an immense increase in freedom of intercourse. His principle was that England had more to gain than any other country by reciprocating facilities. He hoped by a system of preferences to cement our colonies to the mother country, and at the same time to get access on similar terms to the colonial trade of other Powers.

In a somewhat similar spirit Huskisson set aside the prohibitions which had been intended to secure to English silk manufacturers complete possession of the

[1] "I shall think it right to reserve a power of making an addition of one-fifth to the proposed duties, upon the productions of those countries which may refuse, upon a tender by us of the like advantages, to place our commerce and navigation upon the footing of the most favoured nation." *Speeches*, II. 349.

[2] See below, p. 68.

home market, but he gave them advantages of another
kind for competing with foreigners. He reduced the
duties on the raw materials of the manufacture, and
he hoped that with this encouragement they would
be able to hold their own. The woollen and iron
manufactures were similarly treated. He broke down
the monopoly, for he was a believer in the bracing
effects of rivalry, but he fully recognised that it was
advisable to use the tariff—as had been done by
Walpole—as a means of encouraging home industry.

Other changes associated with his name were
made in connection with the collection of revenue;
he took the first steps in a series of measures which
brought our fiscal system into accord with modern
commercial requirements; the work he began was
carried on by Peel, and later by Gladstone. The
method of obtaining revenue from customs, which
was in vogue in 1820, sinned both against the
maxims of "convenience" and "inexpensiveness";
it put merchants to a vast amount of trouble, and the
whole cost to the public was very large in proportion
to the net amount received by Government. Huskisson simplified the tariff by reorganising the
management, while he greatly reduced the rates on
some commodities in the hope that this simplification
and lightening of the burdens would stimulate trade.

Sir Robert Peel's budget of 1842 followed on the
same lines as Huskisson's experiment; but it had an
entirely different character, since the direct encouragement of English industrial prosperity was abandoned.
He relied on the principle that a diminution of duties

would stimulate the volume of trade and eventually
produce a larger customs revenue, even though the rate
charged was reduced. In 1842, when the financial prospects of the country were very gloomy, as we seemed to
have reached the limit of profitable taxation, he boldly
abandoned a large number of very unprofitable items,
and reduced the customs on other commodities; there
was an abatement of duty on 750 articles. Peel was
clear that the real remedy for bad times lay in
stimulating the volume of trade; and though the
effect was not immediate, the results soon shewed
that he had been right, foreign trade increased at the
rate of £4,300,000 a year[1]. English trade in 1842
and in 1853 was capable of rapid expansion; a policy
which would have been impracticable in the days of
domestic manufacture had become possible. The
reduction of duties was followed by such an increase
in the quantities exported and imported that the
revenue from customs increased, while the benefit to
trade[2] was incalculable.

It was of course obvious both to Peel and
Gladstone that, however confidently they might

[1] Cunningham, *Growth of English Industry*, II. 838.

[2] The attitude which Cobden took towards these tariff changes
is one of the proofs that he was more interested in the political
than in the economic aspects of the controversies in which he
engaged. He seems to have been quite indifferent to the immense
reform which was introduced, and only to have calculated that the
temporary measure which accompanied it would be likely to cost
Peel some votes. "I fully expect it will do much to render Peel
unpopular with the upper portion of the middle class, who will see
no compensation in the tariff for a tax upon their incomes and
profits." Morley, *Life of Cobden*, I. 240.

count on the ultimate success of their system, it would be necessary to face a temporary loss[1]. They were bold enough to face this temporary loss quite deliberately ; they felt that the ultimate object made it worth while to take this risk, and that the wise course was to provide against the temporary loss, so that it should not cause serious difficulty when it occurred. With this view they imposed an income-tax as a temporary expedient, and it served its purpose. It enabled these ministers to put the finances of the country on a sounder footing, by readjusting the tariff to suit the commercial requirements of the day, and they did it so prudently that the transition was effected without any serious reduction of income, or dislocation of the administration.

[1] See below, p. 146.

CHAPTER III.

PEEL AND RESTRICTIVE REGULATIONS.

SIR Robert Peel occupies a very special place in the history of the Free Trade movement. We have already seen in what a thoroughgoing fashion he carried through the changes which had been begun under Huskisson in regard to the revenue system. He was, when occasion arose, equally decided in discarding the old policy of the country with regard to the national food supply and the mercantile marine. Unlike Huskisson, he had no scruple in applying the new economic principles. As Cobden observed, "He was peculiarly a politico-economical...intellect[1]." He had adopted a definite doctrine of the currency[2], and tried to put it into effect in the Bank Charter Act of 1844. It was quite in accordance with his habit of mind that he should prefer to carry out the Free Trade principles in their logical completeness, as soon as this course was feasible, rather than attempt any sort

[1] Morley, *Life of Cobden*, I. 237.
[2] McLeod, *Theory and Practice of Banking*, II. 338.

4—2

of compromise. Peel accepted the maxims of economic science as the pronouncements of a master whose
guidance might be followed unhesitatingly[1]. In the
decade from 1840 to 1850 there was a conjunction of
circumstances which made it possible for him to give
effect to his views, and to shape the general economic
policy of the country in accordance with scientific
opinion. The main battle was fought over the
question of mending or ending the Corn Laws.

i.   *The Corn Laws in the Eighteenth Century.*

The protection of tillage had been a feature of the
English system of developing national resources for
centuries. It can be traced back to the times of
rural disorganisation in the fifteenth century, when
sheep-farming was specially profitable, and the progress of enclosure and depopulation was regarded as
a serious evil which it was necessary to check. The
systematic adoption of this scheme may, however, be
dated at the passing of the Corn Bounty Act in 1689.
The Tories would have been glad to see the pressure
of the land-tax reduced; the Whigs preferred the
more enterprising policy of attempting to stimulate
agricultural production, so that the landed interest
might be better able to meet the demands made upon
them. But this Act was not by any means a mere
class measure; in the then conditions of the country
there was good reason to believe that England might

[1] See below, pp. 125—132.

once again become a granary for the less favoured continental lands, as she had been in Roman times, and that improved cultivation would enable us to carry on some branches of commerce to greater advantage. Those who disapprove of the policy of this measure have been able to shew that it had very little, if any, effect, in rendering the price of corn low. It should be noted, however, that this is not the criterion by which the success of the Act of 1689 should be judged. Its authors and advocates desired that the price of corn should be steady, and that it should be remunerative to those engaged in agricultural improvement. There is a mass of evidence which goes to shew that these results were attained during this period.

In 1773 a change took place. The consumption of corn in England seems to have increased so much that, in spite of the larger area which had come into cultivation, the home supply was no longer adequate to the demand in unfavourable years. An ingenious scheme was framed by Governor Pownall, who hoped that it might be possible to keep the price of corn steady, at a somewhat lower rate, by relying partly on homegrown and partly on imported grain. His scheme for supplementing our own production by importation was adopted in 1773, but it did not prove very successful, and before twenty years were over it had broken down altogether. There was a succession of bad seasons in the beginning of the last decade of the eighteenth century; the home supply was very short; but the difficulties of trans-shipment

were so great, that the amount imported was quite
inadequate to relieve the distress. Under the circumstances the Government thought it necessary to grant
subventions to merchants[1], to induce them to import
corn on a large scale, and to such an extent that the
price might fall. The recurring necessity of employing
public money in this fashion gave rise to much
discussion. Would it not be wiser to revert to the
Whig policy of encouraging the improvement of land
and stimulating native production? Sir John Sinclair
argued that internal improvements are "infinitely
superior, in point of solid profit, to that which foreign
commerce produces. In the one case, lists of numerous
vessels loaded with foreign commodities, and the
splendid accounts transmitted from the Custom
House, dazzle and perplex the understanding,
whereas in the other case the operation goes on slowly
but surely. The nation finds itself rich and happy;
and too often attributes that wealth and prosperity
to foreign commerce and distant possessions, which
properly ought to be placed to the account of internal
industry and exertion[2]." The new Corn Law, which
was passed with the view of meeting the home demand
by giving producers the steady encouragement of the
higher price, put a prohibitory duty on the import of
corn unless the price rose above 54/-. How this
scheme might have answered under ordinary circumstances it is impossible to say. The conditions of
English economic life were quite abnormal during the

---

[1] *Reports to House of Commons* (*Reprints*), IX. 45, 49 (1795).
[2] *Reports to House of Commons* (*Reprints*), IX. 209.

Napoleonic wars ; England was so far cut off from the Baltic trade that she had to rely principally on her own production ; great efforts were made to wring sufficient from the soil, and the area under cultivation was much increased. The price of wheat continued to advance, and the agricultural interest began to treat the higher range as something that could be counted upon. Rents were calculated on the new basis ; while the burden of rates—which was augmented by the practice of granting allowances to supplement wages—was only tolerable because of the high prices which could be secured. In 1815, when peace was declared, it became probable that corn would be suddenly poured into England from many places, and that the price would fall enormously ; and this seemed to portend the ruin of the agricultural interests ; it certainly meant the collapse of the system which had been created during the period of unhealthy inflation. The complete ruin of the landed interest would be serious at any time, but it seemed at that juncture an overwhelming catastrophe. The tenant farmers would be the first to suffer ; but the labourers were dependent on the rates, which were borne by the landed interest, and the contributions of the landed gentry to general taxation were very large. Under the circumstances it was plausible, though there were some vigorous protests[1] against

---

[1] The most notable was that of Lord King and other peers ; the fourth paragraph runs thus :—" Whatever may be the future consequences of this law at some future, distant and uncertain period, we see with pain that these hopes must be purchased at the expense

the mistake, to try to avoid sudden and widespread
disaster by attempting to maintain in time of peace
the special conditions which had been created by the
war. The Corn Law of 1815 proceeded on the lines
which had been adopted in 1791 ; but the price at
which importation became easy was fixed at 80/-
instead of 54/-. In this way it was hoped that the
anticipated ruin of the agricultural districts would be
prevented. But whatever excuses there may have
been for it, the proposal was a grave mistake ; in the
eighteenth century the Mercantile System had been
an all-round system, in which careful account had
been taken of the interaction of various parts for
the benefit of Great Britain and the British revenue as
a whole. The Corn Law of 1815 was, as experience
soon demonstrated, a class measure, by which one
section of the community was protected at the
expense of other sections, and to the disadvantage of
the whole.

of a great and present evil. To compel the consumer to purchase
corn dearer at home than it might be imported from abroad is the
immediate practical effect of this law ; in this way alone can it
operate; its present protection, its promised extension of agriculture,
must result (if at all) from the profits which it creates by keeping
up the price of corn to an artificial level: these future benefits are
the consequences expected, but as we confidently believe, errone-
ously expected, from giving a bounty to the grower of corn, by
a tax levied on its consumer." J. E. T. Rogers, *Protests of Lords*,
II. 482. Compare also Lord King's *Short History of the Job of
Jobs* written in 1825.

ii. *The failure of the Corn Law of* 1815.

It is unnecessary for our purpose to spend time over the modifications which were introduced into the measure of 1815, in 1828 and 1842, as there was no substantial change of policy : the strenuous effort to keep the price of corn high and steady, with the view of maintaining an artificially forced system of agricultural production, proved, after being tried for twenty years, to be a disastrous failure.

The strongest grounds on which the measure had been advocated were political; great advantage would doubtless have accrued from anything which should have rendered this country self-sufficing, and independent of the risk of having to rely on an imported food supply. This highly protective measure did not, however, serve to call forth a sufficient production from the soil of the United Kingdom. Enough corn was not grown to meet the requirements of the population, and it was necessary after all to import a considerable quantity. The experiment was crucial ; a highly protective tariff did not and could not render Great Britain self-sufficing ; we must rely on the extension of our commerce and the maintenance of our supremacy at sea for a large portion of the corn which is necessary for our population. That point was settled finally, and by experience.

The economic results of the measure were equally disappointing ; the price of corn was not kept high. The average price during this period was much lower than it had been during the Napoleonic wars, and

very little higher than it became when the Corn Laws
were repealed. Though prices varied greatly under
the law, they did not range very high on the whole;
but the fluctuations were injurious to the steady
prosecution of tillage. The landlords demanded
high rents, which occasional high prices seemed to
justify; but the tenants could not afford to pay
them regularly, and in successive decades the farmers
were in serious difficulties. In good years the farmer
made no profit because prices were low; and the
system of parish allowances gave an excuse for keeping wages down at a starvation level. The landowners and tithe-owners benefited by their monopoly
of the home production, but the other elements in the
agricultural interest derived no appreciable advantages
from legislative protection. It was only with the
introduction of scientific methods, about 1836, that
farming became remunerative.

While the law of 1815 failed to secure the good
results which had been anticipated, it proved posi-
tively mischievous in its effects on English commerce
and industry. The development of trade with the
Baltic lands and the United States of America was
seriously restricted. Grain was the product which
they could most easily send in return for our manufactures. If corn had been habitually accepted in
payment for goods, more English shipping would
have been employed, and much larger amounts of
English wares would have been sold in foreign markets.
Hence the effect of agricultural protection was to
injure the industrial classes. This was brought about

through the indirect limitation of the employment of our shipping and artisans rather than by any direct influence exercised in raising the price of food.

Other secondary results gave rise to some anxiety; the first suspicion that England might be ousted from her position of workshop of the world began to make itself felt. Economists argued that since foreign countries were precluded from buying our manufactures with their products, they were being forced in self-defence to try and supply themselves with hardware and textiles as best they could. Foreign competition with our industries was being galvanised into existence by protective tariffs, and this was alleged to be a retaliation for the protection of English agriculture. Foreign countries might have been willing to cooperate with England in an exchange of products and wares on equal terms, but, as it was alleged, our unwillingness to buy their grain aroused their determination to supply themselves with home-made goods.

Looking back from this distance of time, we cannot but feel that the case against the existing Corn Law was overwhelming. The agitation against it was taken up with great vigour by the Anti-Corn-Law League, which was founded in 1838, and reconstituted in 1839. It was admirably organised, and the campaign was conducted with great energy and skill. Cobden, as a country-bred boy, was able to carry on the war in rural districts with success, by shewing the farmers that protection had not actually given them real help, but that numbers had been ruined in the effort to maintain the cultivation of the land. The appeal to the interests of the commercial classes and the manufacturers was more positive; they were ready to be persuaded that agricultural protection had been a barrier to promoting the free expansion of commerce and industry. On one point Cobden was careful; he would not promise that the repeal of the Corn Laws would introduce an era of cheap food. This line Sir Robert Peel was ready to take, but Cobden repudiated it. "Assuredly," he said, "the Prime Minister took the least comprehensive or statesmanlike view of his measures when he proposed to degrade prices, instead of aiming to sustain them by enlarging the circle of exchange[1]." Whatever the expectations of other manufacturers may have been, Cobden's language on this point was so carefully guarded, that it is possible to repel the charge which was made by the Socialists. Karl Marx contended that the English employers, who favoured the repeal of the Corn Laws, were actuated by a desire to make food cheap[2], in the expectation

---

[1] 12 March, 1844, *Speeches*, I. 143.

[2] "But, strange to say, the people for whom cheap food is to be procured at all costs are very ungrateful. Cheap food is as ill-reputed in England as is cheap government in France. The people see in these self-sacrificing gentlemen, in Bowring, Bright and Company, their worst enemies and most shameless hypocrites....

"The manufacturer turns his back upon the working men and replies to the shopkeeper: 'As to that, you leave it to us! Once rid of the duty on corn we shall import cheaper corn from abroad. Then we shall reduce wages at the very time when they are rising in the countries where we get our corn. Thus, in addition to the advantages which we already enjoy we shall have lower wages

that if food were cheaper they would be able to force down wages to a lower level and establish a more complete tyranny over the hands. The hostility of Lancashire employers to the Factory Acts gave an impression that they were at heart indifferent to the welfare of the operatives, and it was easy to represent their enthusiasm for cheap food as inspired by a desire to reduce the expenses of production. It is at all events clear that the forebodings of the Socialists have not been realised; but it is also clear that the criticism could not apply to a man like Cobden, who did not anticipate that the repeal of the Corn Law would lead to a substantial lowering of the price of corn. He insisted that the poor would be benefited even if bread maintained its price; he argued that a very large part of the population were half-starved for want of means of buying bread; he held that the repeal of the Corn Laws would entail, not merely a larger supply of corn, but more regular employment, so that the demand would be increased, because more people would be able to pay for as much food as they needed at the current rates. A large supply would be forthcoming from abroad and from home, but the price need not fall if, as he believed, the people were better able to pay.

and, with all these advantages we shall easily force the Continent to buy of us.'

"The English working men have appreciated to the fullest extent the significance of the struggle between the lords of the land and of capital. They know very well that the price of bread was to be reduced in order to reduce wages, and that the profit of capital would rise by as much as rent fell." K. Marx. *Speech before the Democratic Club*, Brussels, 9th January, 1848.

iii. *The occasion of the repeal.*

Considering the excellence of their organisation, the strength of their case, and the vigour with which it was presented, we cannot but be surprised that the Anti-Corn-Law League made so little apparent progress in the first six years of their existence. In the early part of 1845 the League were spending £1,000 a week; but, as Mr Morley says, " In spite of the activity which was involved in these profuse supplies, the outlook of the cause was perhaps never less hopeful or encouraging. The terrible depression which had at first given so poignant an impulse to the agitation had vanished. Peel's manipulations of the tariff had done something to bring about a revival of trade; much more had been done by two magnificent harvests[1]," and under these circumstances the country was indisposed to make any revolutionary changes. But the public temper was deeply affected by the disastrous summer and autumn of 1845. " It was the wettest autumn in the memory of man, and the rain came over the hills in a downpour that never ceased by night or by day. It was the rain that rained away the Corn Laws[2]." The scarcity which was threatened in England became a disastrous famine in Ireland, where the potato crop was ruined by disease. Under the strain of this exceptional demand for foreign food some relaxation of the Corn Law became inevitable, and any relaxation was

---

[1] Morley, *Life of Cobden*, I. 312.
[2] Morley, *Life of Cobden*, I. 334.

in reality an admission that the system had been a failure. The fruit of the agitation by the Anti-Corn-Law League was seen at last; their argument had affected public opinion so much that there was no prospect of framing a compromise which could be regarded as acceptable. First Lord John Russell and then Sir Robert Peel declared in favour of the policy of abandoning agricultural protection. The former failed to form an administration in December 1845; and Peel found himself deserted by many of his party when he moved his Resolutions in January 1846. The policy of Free Trade was accepted by Parliament, not because a majority of either House was convinced of the soundness of the economic principles, and the wisdom of adopting them, but because there seemed to be no other obvious solution for the difficulties of the moment; the new proposal received an unwilling assent, which was extorted from a Parliament that had received a mandate to maintain the established system[1].

This great decision was taken, not only suddenly, but under the influence of some serious misapprehensions. The economists and politicians of 1846 had no idea of the manner in which the new facilities for communication, by means of steamers and railroads, would affect the British farmer. They assumed that he enjoyed a natural protection, both as regards corn growing and stock breeding, and that it was absurd to suppose his business would prove less profitable, at all events in the hands of capable men with sufficient

[1] Morley, *Life of Cobden*, I. 348.

capital. McCulloch had been very explicit on the probable effects of removing the restrictions on the importation of foreign cattle and greatly reducing the duty on corn.

"Is it not the extreme of childishness to suppose that the value of stock is to be seriously depressed and the breeders and graziers ruined, by the purposed relaxation of restrictions on importation from abroad? It is singular how in a great and rich country like this a vast addition may be made to the supply of any important article without materially affecting prices....It is much to be regretted that the same manly and decisive course was not taken in respect of corn that is proposed to be taken in respect of butchers' meat. The delusion in the one case is quite as great as in the other. Suppose the ports were constantly open to importation at a fixed duty of 5/- a quarter on wheat, it admits of demonstration that our average prices would not thereby be in the least degree affected. But such a measure would have given us an additional security against the mischievous effects of bad harvests, at the same time that it would have made an end of a gigantic delusion, and have dried up a most prolific source of misrepresentation, abuse, and agitation[1]." Cobden was even more precise. "The truth is that you all know— that the country knows—that there never was a more monstrous delusion than to suppose that that which goes to increase the trade of the country, and

[1] McCulloch. *Memorandums on the proposed importation of foreign beef and live stock* (1842), p. 9.

to extend its manufactures and commerce—that which adds to our numbers, increases our population, enlarges the number of your customers, and diminishes your burdens by multiplying the shoulders that are to bear them, and giving them increased strength to bear them—can possibly tend to diminish the value of land[1]." It has now become clear that on this point the great leader of the agitation, like the most eminent economist of the day, was under a misapprehension as to the effect of the course which he recommended so vigorously.

Business men were also inclined to overestimate the stability of the industrial supremacy of Great Britain. They might no longer take the supercilious view in regard to the nascent American manufactures, which was possible in 1797, nor display the easy confidence in the practical monopoly of mechanical appliances which they possessed in 1820; but it was supposed that foreign industries were for the most part exotic, that they had been artificially nurtured[2], and that, with a fair field and no favour, the English manufacturers could command the markets of the world. They would not have dreamt that in little more than half a century America would greatly outstrip England in the production of pig-iron, or that Germany would pass us in any branch of an international industrial competition.

These misapprehensions in regard to the probable future of British agriculture and industry were very

---

[1] 27 February, 1846. *Speeches*, I. 382.
[2] *Edinburgh Review*, 1820, XXXIII. 339.

excusable, but they were none the less real; and the same may be said about the anticipations which were expressed in regard to the probable action of other countries. Peel himself, like the London merchants of 1820, was convinced on economic principles that insular Free Trade was expedient for England; but he felt that he could not count upon the House of Commons to endorse this view, and in presenting his resolutions on January 27th, 1846, he laboured to shew that there were everywhere signs—in the United States, Naples, Norway, Sweden, Austria, and Hanover—of a willingness to follow our example, if we once took the plunge. A fortnight before this date, and while it was still uncertain what precise course Sir Robert Peel would propose in Parliament, Cobden had uttered his celebrated prediction: " I believe that if you abolish the Corn Law honestly, and adopt Free Trade in its simplicity, there will not be a tariff in Europe that will not be changed in less than five years to follow your example[1]."

This forecast of the great organiser and the Prime Minister was a highly reasonable one ; there was much to be said in its favour, but subsequent events have proved it mistaken. The fact remains that Peel, like Cobden, was under a misapprehension in regard to the prospective action of other countries when he advocated the repeal of the Corn Laws in the House of Commons.

---

[1] January 15, 1846. *Speeches*, I. 360.

iv. *The results of the repeal.*

The measures for regulating the food supply of
the country had been one part of a long-established
system of economic policy ; but when this plank was
cut away the whole fabric collapsed.   The protection
of native industry had been accepted as a sound
principle from time immemorial ; and Huskisson had
borne it in mind throughout his reforms ; but Peel
discarded it altogether.   It was not merely that he
saw that industrial protection could not be maintained
after the repeal of the Corn Laws; he held that, both
as regards manufactures and agriculture, protective
duties were "not in themselves abstractedly good and
ought to be relinquished[1]."   At the same time a very
serious blow was struck at the system of encouraging
colonial development which had been devised by
Huskisson.   Canada had enjoyed a considerable
preference over the United States for shipping wheat
to Great Britain ; but the Act of 1846, which swept
away the duties imposed on imported corn, abolished
the advantage she had possessed[2].   The Free Trade
movement placed the colonists economically in the
same position as foreigners ; it gave them scope
eventually for claiming the right to manage their
own affairs in entire independence of the mother
country, but this political advantage did not com-

[1] June 27, 1846. 3 *Hansard*, LXXXIII. 241.
[2] According to the Act of 1842, when corn was selling at 58s.
Canadian wheat paid 1s. and wheat from the States 14s. duty.

pensate them for the immediate economic loss, or for
the wounded feeling which was engendered by the
slight concern of Great Britain with regard to their
interests[1].

The effort to maintain the maritime power of
the country had been the very foundation of the
Mercantile System; and within five years of the repeal
of the Corn Laws, the measures which had been
devised for fostering British shipping were given up.
The Navigation Acts, as modified by Huskisson, had
been the subject of enquiry by a Royal Commission
and had been codified in 1845 ; but the causes which
had brought about the repeal of the Corn Laws put
an entirely new complexion on the matter.   During
the Irish famine, temporary permission had been given
to import food stuffs from the United States, and
American exporters had been able to use both
American and British ships, while the Canadians
complained that they were compelled to pay higher

[1] Davidson, *Commercial Federation*, 47.

The point was insisted on in the House of Commons during a
discussion on the Navigation Act.   Mr C. Anstey protested against
the system of the Free Trade School,...and thought the colonies
ought to be legislated for as an integral portion of the British
Empire.   He said that Mr J. Hume "seemed now to lament the
discontent of the colonies, and to set a high value on their connection, forgetting that it was the darling theory of the Free Trade
school that the colonies were useless, and that the sooner they were
shaken off the better.   The reason why so much discontent existed
in the colonies was, because the Government forced their Free
Trade measures upon the colonists contrary to their wishes and
their interests; and the Colonial Office was as ardent in enforcing
the adoption of those doctrines as the colonists were zealous to
resist them."   16th April, 1849.   3 *Hansard*, CIV. 367.

freights, because they were restricted to British shipping. Several representations were made on this subject; and the West Indian colonists had similar grievances in regard to the existing laws. At the juncture when the question was raised, as to readjusting the regulations or sweeping them away altogether, there could be no doubt which course would carry the day. No effort was made by the ministers in power to give effect to the modifications which would have met the views of the colonists; they acted on the *doctrinaire* principle in disregard of the warning of practical men[1]. In 1849 the shipping interest, like

[1] In the light of after events the discussions in both Houses of Parliament are instructive. The protest of Lord Stanley (afterwards Earl of Derby) gives a good summary of the case against the Bill.

"1st. Because the Bill, while professing to amend the laws for the encouragement of British shipping and navigation, virtually repeals those laws under the protection of which the mercantile marine of this country has attained its present eminence.

"2ndly. Because such repeal was not called for by any State necessity nor by public opinion, which, on the contrary, has manifested itself universally and unequivocally as hostile to the measure.

"3rdly. Because any minor inconveniences to which British commerce may be subjected by the operation of the existing laws might easily have been obviated by modifications and amendments not inconsistent with the maintenance of their general principle.

"4thly. Because the Bill fails to secure to the shipping and commerce of this country in foreign ports advantages equivalent to those which it confers upon the shipping of foreign countries.

"5thly. Because it surrenders gratuitously, and without any possible equivalent, to all foreign countries, the trade between the United Kingdom and its widely spread colonies and dependencies, in which trade a very large proportion of our shipping and seamen is constantly and profitably employed.

"6thly. Because by the concession of the indirect carrying trade

tillage and manufacturing, and colonial development,
was left to take care of itself, and the policy of the
Navigation Acts was abandoned. The victory of the
Free Trade movement had been as complete as it was

between the United Kingdom and all foreign ports, any one nation
which may be able to rival us in building, manning, and sailing
ships, will be enabled to enter into successful competition with us
throughout the world, and thus lay the foundation of a maritime
superiority which it is essential to this country to retain, and which
it was the especial object of the Navigation Laws to prevent any
foreign powers from acquiring.

"7thly. Because the Bill directly encourages the competition
of foreign labour, and tends to diminish the demand for British
seamen, British shipwrights, mechanics, and artisans, unduly to
lower the amount of their wages, and greatly to discourage the
employment of British industry.

"8thly. Because the permission to register as British, ships
built in foreign ports, will inevitably lead to a great transfer of
capital to those foreign ports, and to the infliction of serious injury
upon the ship-building establishments of this country, and the
various branches of industry connected therewith, by which, in
time of peace, employment is given to large numbers of our fellow-
subjects, and the assistance of which, in time of war, has been
found indispensable to the maintenance of the strength and efficiency
of the Royal Navy.

"9thly. Because the Bill, by exposing British ship-owners to
unlimited competition with those of foreign countries, while it leaves
them subject to restrictions from which their rivals are exempt,
holds out strong inducements to them to sail under a foreign flag,
with foreign-built ships, and foreign seamen, to the manifest injury
of the best interests of the country.

"10thly. Because the Royal Navy is mainly dependent for its
efficiency upon the commercial marine and the classes of the community connected therewith; and this Bill, by discouraging the employment of British ship-builders, ships, and seamen, tends directly to
the reduction of the commercial marine, and thereby to the diminution of that naval strength which is the main foundation of the
greatness of this country and the surest defence of its independence."
Protests of the Lords, III. 361.

sudden; both parties in the State had become committed to it, almost against their will. The general election of 1852 was a plebiscite which endorsed the action that had been taken; and this was accepted by Disraeli as a final verdict in regard to the Elizabethan system of protection.

For a quarter of a century the economic results which followed the adoption of Free Trade continued to confirm the advocates of the change and their followers in their conviction as to the wisdom of the revolution effected in 1846. Circumstances of many kinds conspired to afford England a period of unexampled national progress.

The forecast of Cobden as to the effect on rural districts appeared to be completely fulfilled. High farming was prosecuted in many areas; and though prices ranged a little lower, the English grower was not seriously affected by foreign competition. This was not due to his "natural protection" being adequate, but to the fact that there were other causes which handicapped foreign producers. The Crimean War had cut off the Russian supplies for a time; the American Civil War delayed the opening up of that country; till early in the Seventies it was true to say that British agriculture had prospered under the policy of Free Trade.

Of English industry this was still more strikingly true; there were many conditions, altogether independent of the change of policy, which co-operated to cause it to advance by leaps and bounds. The gold discoveries in California and Australia stimulated commercial activity in all parts of the world, and the commercial supremacy of England enabled her to gain a large share of this increased trade. The general introduction of railway and steamship communication gave increased facilities for traffic, and these new conditions had a favourable reaction on industry. How much of the progress was due to one, and how much to another factor, it is impossible to say; but twenty-five years after the change, no one could deny that English commerce and industry had prospered under the Free Trade policy.

When the country was viewed in its social aspects it was also clear that things were going well, according to the test which the Mercantile System had most conspicuously failed to satisfy[1]. The welfare of the working classes of the community had become much more assured; the skilled artisans had risen out of the desperate straits to which so many of them had been reduced, and the agricultural and unskilled labourers were participating in the advantages of higher wages and better conditions of life. The fear that cheaper food would be a step in the further degradation of labour had been wholly illusory; the working classes had had somewhat cheaper food, and they had at the same time gained enormously in status. In this matter, too, there had of course been co-operating causes, quite unconnected with the new economic policy. The great scheme of poor law reform, which had been based on the enquiries of the Royal Commission of 1833, had come into full

[1] See p. 37 above.

operation in 1845; the freedom which had been given to Trades Unions to exist, by the repeal of the Combination Acts in 1825, had been gradually used, so that artisan opinion was organised; and the Reform Bill of 1867 had given them an effective voice in the shaping of legislation. It is not easy to see that any of the steps of social advance, except the last, were due to the new policy in regard to food, but they had at all events been compatible with it.

The constitutional changes which occurred during this period were, on the other hand, very directly connected with the Free Trade movement. Much had been done to break down the monopoly of power which had been possessed by the landed gentry before Cobden entered on political life. The Reform Bill of 1832 had enfranchised the great industrial centres, and the Municipal Corporations Act had introduced a new era of self-government in the towns. But these great changes had fallen very flat[1]; the classes who had hitherto possessed exclusive rights still retained the practical power; the formulæ of Radicals and the aspirations of the various groups of Socialists seemed to be entirely in the air. Cobden aimed at giving these opinions a practical turn, and he succeeded. He brought the scattered elements together and rallied them round the question of the Corn Laws.[2] Ideals and sentiments were successfully linked with economic interests, and thus he obtained a political organisation which was

[1] Morley, *Life of Cobden*, I. 89.
[2] Morley, *Life of Cobden*, I. 126. See page 171 below.

strong enough to secure a victory. The triumph of Radicalism, under Cobden's astute guidance, was the last step in the work of transforming our Constitution, so that it should harmonise with the requirements of a great commercial community. Commerce and industry, rather than land, had become the chief factors in the economic prosperity of the country; and the oligarchy which raised England to such a high position among the nations was at length superseded by a democracy which has been thoroughly aroused to a consciousness of its power.

CHAPTER IV.

COBDEN AND COMMERCIAL TREATIES.

i. *The culminating point of progress.*

RICHARD COBDEN had succeeded in using the Free
Trade movement as an instrument for placing the
effective government of England on a democratic
basis ; but he was still more enthusiastic about the
results which might be expected from the progress of
this economic doctrine in the sphere of international
politics.   He believed that, if the various nations
would only agree to allow full commercial intercourse,
an era of universal peace would necessarily ensue.
Free Trade seemed to him to be a healing medicine
which would allay political ambitions and national
rivalries.   He stated this explicitly in a letter written
in 1842.   " It has struck me that it would be well
to try to engraft our Free Trade agitation upon the
Peace movement.   They are one and the same cause.
It has often been to me a matter of the greatest surprise, that the Friends have not taken up the question
of Free Trade as the means—and I believe the only

human means—of effecting universal and permanent peace. The efforts of the Peace Societies, however laudable, can never be successful so long as the nations maintain their present system of isolation. The colonial system, with all its dazzling appeals to the passions of the people, can never be got rid of except by the indirect process of Free Trade, which will gradually and imperceptibly loose the bands which unite the Colonies to us by a mistaken notion of self-interest. Yet the Colonial policy of Europe has been the chief source of wars for the last hundred and fifty years. Again, Free Trade, by perfecting the intercourse and securing the dependence of countries upon one another, must inevitably snatch the power from the *governments* to plunge their people into wars[1]." This ideal had an intense fascination for Cobden; he was one of "those who from politico-economical and financial considerations are not only the advocates of peace, but also of a diminution of our costly peace establishments[2]." He believed that the diffusion of Free Trade principles was the only practical method of bringing about the realisation of this hope.

His conviction as to the efficacy of this means was in complete accord with his ordinary habit of mind on economic and political subjects. He was inclined to assume that economic conditions are the determining cause of political changes; and the history of England during the preceding half century gave

[1] Morley, *Life of Cobden*, I. 230.
[2] Morley, *Life of Cobden*, II. 144.

ample confirmation of this view. In particular he held that economic dependence is the best guarantee for political alliance[1]. According to Cobden, increased facilities for commerce would make the consumers in each country realise how much they gained by trade, and render them jealous of any governmental action that might interrupt it. Each year's experience of any arrangement for freeing commerce was a pledge of further progress in the same direction. It thus came about that Cobden was entirely an opportunist in endeavouring to promote free intercourse; and that at length in 1860 he separated himself from those who were Free Traders on principle since they deprecated measures which could not be defended as practical applications of the doctrine of unfettered exchange. In 1843 Cobden had voted with the advocates of insular Free Trade against Peel, who was at that time in favour of gradually enlarging the circle of intercourse by means of treaties with other Powers. When ten years had elapsed, from the period of repeal, and other nations had not followed the English example, Cobden began to hesitate as to the course which should be pursued;

[1] To this opinion experience was not altogether favourable. The Tory party from time immemorial had aimed at rendering the American colonies economically dependent on England; but the measures taken with this object had not served to cement the attachment of the colonists to Great Britian. It is, however, possible to draw a distinction and urge that a forced dependence had strained allegiance, but that voluntary interdependence will be mutually beneficial, and will tend to strengthen the alliance of two friendly peoples.

he definitely broke with the economic experts who
believed that the principle of free intercourse was
certain to appeal to rational minds sooner or later.
He felt that it was useless to appeal to the French
to modify their tariffs on grounds of pure reason, not
because of any insular contempt for the French, but
because no country ever had been convinced by such
reasoning. Peel had been converted by it, but no
other responsible statesman had been carried away
by it, and England had required other arguments[1].

Cobden looked back on the careful strategy and the
pressure of starvation by the help of which victory had
been secured in England, and he was not surprised that
the French were slow in accepting our policy. He felt
that we must meet them half way, and thus in 1859
he fell in with the project of securing increased opportunities for foreign trade by means of commercial
treaties. In taking this line he had the cordial
support of Mr Gladstone, who stated his view very
forcibly. "I understand the statement of the
moderate Free Trader who says that half a loaf is
better than no bread, that all breaking down of
restrictions is good, and that it is wiser to break
down our own restrictions and leave those of our

[1] Morley, *Life of Cobden*, II. 339. "These people seem to think
that Free Trade in France can be carried by a logical, orderly,
methodical process, without resorting to stratagem, or anything like
an indirect proceeding. They forget the political plots and con-
trivances, and the fearful adjuncts of starvation, which were
necessary for carrying similar measures in England. They forget
how Free Trade was wrested from the reluctant majorities of both
our Houses of Parliament."

neighbour standing if we cannot touch them, than to perpetuate both. That is true and reasonable; but I cannot understand those immoderate and unmanageable Free Traders, who come from other quarters, many of whom have not long been thus fastidious and jealous on behalf of Free Trade in its most rigid purity, and who seem to think it is a positive evil to induce our neighbours to break down their restrictions. They do not see that what they condemn is a doubling of the benefit. They think there is a chivalry in Free Trade, which is degraded if it becomes a matter of bargain, whereas it appears to me that bargain is really the true end and aim of the whole[1]."

Though the Free Trade movement had not made such progress as Cobden anticipated, it was clearly in the ascendant; there was an active propaganda in its favour both in America and France. Opinion in the United States appeared to be trending in this direction; the tide seemed to have turned. The policy of protecting American manufactures had been adopted in 1816[2], and was vigorously pursued till at length the 'Abomination of 1828' was passed. In 1831 and 1833 a reaction set in; and in 1846 a much more liberal tariff was introduced, while an important manifesto was issued by Mr Walker, the Secretary to the Treasury, setting forth the Free Trade principles and urging their adoption by the

---

[1] 10 Feb., 1860. 3 *Hansard*, CLVI. 842.

[2] Rabbeno, *American Commercial Policy*, 155. This was apparently in retaliation for the Corn Law of 1815. Shortt, *Imperial Preferential Trade*, 33.

United States[1]. From this period until the very eve
of the Civil War[2] there seemed to be good reason to
suppose that the Americans were becoming more
prepared to follow the English lead and abandon
protection altogether.

The doctrine of Free Trade appeared also to be
gaining ground in France. The tradition of French
economic science as established by Turgot was maintained by a new generation, among whom Bastiat—
an intimate friend of Cobden's—took a prominent
part. The nation generally was protectionist, but
this academic group had the ear of Government
and exercised an influence out of all proportion to
their numbers. Napoleon III had persuaded himself
that Free Trade was a bold course which it was wise
to adopt; acting as the "organisation of the masses[3],"
in opposition to the organised manufacturers, he was
so far absolute in matters of tariff that he was able
to make the experiment which expert opinion recommended.

Symptoms of the increasing prevalence of Free
Trade ideas could be noticed in other directions
during the Fifties. Austria and Germany included
the territory from the Baltic to the Adriatic in one
system of internal Free Trade. The Zollverein and
Austria entered into very close commercial relations
in 1853[4]; the barriers against the outside world were

---

[1] Quoted by Peel, 3 *Hansard*, LXXXIII. 278.

[2] Rabbeno, *American Commercial Policy*, 200.

[3] Morley, *Life of Cobden*, II. 340.

[4] On the elements which composed the Free Trade party in

maintained, but those which had prevented free intercourse between the German-speaking peoples were greatly reduced. The economic doctrine of Free Trade in one form or another[1] seemed to be steadily winning its way in all the great commercial countries. England had taken the lead, America and France were ready to follow suit, and Austro-Germany was moving in the same direction under Prussian guidance. The progress was not so rapid as had been expected, but though slow there seemed to be good reason to believe it was sure.

The political atmosphere in Europe generally was in many ways congenial to the growth of the international intercourse from which Cobden hoped for so much. The era of International Exhibitions and friendly rivalry in mechanical ingenuity was inaugurated in Hyde Park in 1851; it was a monumental protest against militarism which found an echo on many sides. The Radicals in England had always insisted that the army and navy were maintained on a large scale in the interest of the classes, for whom they provided pleasant and remunerative posts, and that the welfare of the masses demanded considerable retrenchment. On the Continent, Liberalism—in an academic rather than a party sense— was making rapid progress. The opinion had gained ground that on the whole government is an evil, and that the less there is of it the better; there was a

Germany, and their difference from the English advocates see Lotz, *Die Ideen der deutschen Handelspolitik*, in Leipsic *Schriften des Vereins für Socialpolitik*, L. 13.   [1] *Ibid.* 8.

tendency to limit the range and interference of government as much as possible, so as to leave the fullest freedom for individual action. Liberalism, in this sense, is opposed to Socialism, since one seeks to limit the functions of government, and the other to extend them ; and the attitude of resistance to the ruling authority, rather than dependence upon it, commended itself to some of the popular leaders. The revolutionary movements of 1848 had brought the aspirations for liberty within, and for tranquil relations with neighbours into line. There was a feeling that the wars and quarrels between nations had been dynastic in character and due to the ambition of kings, but that the life of the people was bound up with solid advance in material well-being. These ideas of the brotherhood of nations were favourable to freedom of commercial intercourse, and they were becoming diffused at the time when new facilities for traffic by railway and steamer were coming into general use. Everything seemed propitious for the breaking down of barriers which prevented the industry of the world from being developed in the most suitable circumstances. There was good reason to hope that any country which adopted Free Trade, even temporarily, would find so much benefit from increased commerce that all opposition would ere long be effectually silenced. Such was the position of affairs when Cobden succeeded in passing the commercial treaty with France in 1860.

The Anglo-French Treaty of 1860 was important from the manner in which it enabled each country to participate in the natural advantages of the other; the French opened up their markets to English iron, and French wines were imported in much larger quantities. The main importance of the agreement lay in the fact that it served as a foundation-stone on which a whole fabric of treaties securing greater freedom of commercial intercourse was built up. The treaty contained a most favoured nation clause; according to this England pledged herself not only to lower her duties on French products, but on similar products from other countries, and France made a corresponding engagement. "This was not reciprocity of monopoly, but reciprocity of freedom, or partial freedom. England had given up the system of differential duties, and France knew that the products of every other country would receive at the English ports exactly the same measure of treatment as her own. France, on the other hand, openly intended to take her treaty with England as a model for treaties with the rest of Europe, and to concede by treaty with as many Governments as might wish, a tariff just as favourable as that which had been arranged with England. As a matter of fact within five years of the negotiation of 1860 France had made treaties with Belgium, the Zollverein, Italy, Sweden, Norway, Switzerland, and Austria[1]." These treaties, like another which was subsequently concluded between England and Austria, recognised the "most favoured nation" principle, the "sheet-anchor of Free Trade, as it has been called. By means of

[1] Morley, *Life of Cobden*, II. 341.

this principle, each new point gained in any one
negotiation becomes a part of the common commercial
system of the European confederation. 'By means
of this network,' it had been excellently said by
a distinguished member of the English diplomatic
service, 'of which few Englishmen seem to be aware[1],
while fewer still know to whom they owe it, all the
great trading and industrial communities of Europe
i.e., England, France, Holland, Belgium, the Zollverein
(1870), Austria, and Italy, constitute a compact
international body, from which the principle of
monopoly and exclusive privilege has once for all
been eliminated, and not one member of which can
take off a single duty without all the other members
at once partaking in the increased trading facilities
thereby created. By the self-registering action of the
most favoured nation clause[2], common to this network
of treaties, the tariff level of the whole body is being
continually lowered, and the road being paved towards
the final embodiment of the Free Trade principle in
the international engagement to abolish all duties
other than those levied for revenue purposes[3].' "

It thus came about that during the decade from
1860—1870 the principle of Free Trade was very

---

[1] A further result of this ignorance is that comparatively few
people are aware how far other countries have withdrawn the
facilities for free intercourse which they formerly afforded to
England. Compare Fuchs, *Die Handelspolitik Englands*, 33—65.

[2] Canadian dissatisfaction with the results of Free Trade took
the form of a demand to be consulted in all treaty arrangements
which affected their commerce. Davidson, *Commercial Federation*,
64.

[3] Morley, *Life of Cobden*, II. 342.

generally brought into operation, and there was good reason to hope that the favourable results achieved would soon secure its permanent adoption, not only by the countries which had accepted it tentatively but by all other civilised states.

ii. *The Great Divide.*

During these years when the advocates of Free Trade were able to believe that they were successfully laying the foundations of Universal Peace, there was a considerable recrudescence of militarism both in Europe and America; the economic ties and popular interests were not strong enough to induce the nations to ignore causes of difference; political relationships did not adapt themselves closely to business requirements. Besides the Crimean War there was the War of Italian Independence, in which the Austrians were driven from the valley of the Po, with French help; and the conflicts with Denmark and Austria, which raised Prussia to a position of recognised leadership among the German-speaking peoples. In these cases the Government made itself the leader in giving effect to national aspirations; the revived military spirit was not merely dynastic but democratic. This was still more strikingly true of the contest which had broken out in America; the Northern and Southern States found themselves engaged in a fratricidal struggle, and peace was only declared when the resources of the weaker side were utterly exhausted. The Franco-German War of 1870 gave an object lesson to every country that desires to preserve its national traditions and live an independent life, and forced men to recognise the necessity of being well prepared for war. The fresh development of the national spirit, under new conditions, proved fatal to the continuance of those experiments in Free Trade which had been attempted in so many quarters.

The revival of foreign protection, which became noticeable in the Seventies, was closely connected with these military operations. It is obvious that the expenses of war had to be paid for. In the case of America the customs duties were almost the only source of revenue which was under the authority of the central government; and it was necessary for fiscal purposes to try to obtain the largest possible revenue by means of the tariff. A similar course was approved by M. Thiers, who had always been a convinced protectionist, when he had to administer the affairs of France[1]. Under the Republic the policy embodied in the Cobden Treaty was severely criticised, and in 1882 the agreement was allowed to drop[2]. High tariffs on imported manufactures proved to be a convenient source from which to levy revenue for a country that was exhausted by war.

It would, however, be a mistake to suppose that the return to protection was merely incidental; there was a very deep and close connection between the outburst of militarism and the reversal of economic

---

[1] A. Devers, *La politique commerciale de la France depuis 1866*, in Leipsic *Schriften des Vereins für Socialpolitik*, LI. 155.

[2] *Ibid.* 172.

policy. A rising sense of national self-consciousness uttered itself in both fashions. The desire to organise the economic life of the nation in independence of its neighbours was the expression in another field of the spirit which was ready to fight for national unity. The struggle in the United States had been due to an intense eagerness on the part of the North to stand out to the world, not as a congeries of little republics, but as one polity, with one national system throughout the whole of an immense territory. The contest had been occasioned by the slave question, because slavery was the most important element which severed the Southern from the Northern and Western States; but the enthusiasm for a united polity, that should command the admiration of the world, was the great force which slave-owners brought into play against themselves. Even before the war broke out, the desire to foster national economic development had been making itself felt anew[1]; and under the tariffs, which were introduced for revenue purposes, powerful vested interests sprang up and were able to secure increasing protection for the native producers. A similar result was brought about in France, though by somewhat different stages; the Free Trade experiment had been the policy of the Third Empire; it had never been really popular. When the Empire fell the demand for protection was exceedingly vigorous, as it seemed necessary to take active steps to foster the agriculture and industry of a country exhausted by war. This positive determination to organise the economic life of

---

[1] Rabbeno, *American Commercial Policy*, 200, dates it at 1857.

the nation as a whole, was in flat opposition to Cobden's aspiration after the economic interdependency of nations. That had been tried, partially, and now it was deliberately rejected.

The reaction against Free Trade soon spread to countries which had no special political excuse—in the effects of an exhausting war—for reverting to protection. Germany and Austria each resorted to it, on purely economic grounds, as the best means to increase their resources. German unity had at length been attained, under the guidance of the Prussian monarchs, and German ambition was fired with the desire to exercise a great influence as a world power. Her natural wealth had been left undeveloped to a considerable extent, and she hoped, by protection, not merely to make up the lee-way of centuries of division, but to build up great industries and establish a world-wide commerce; the first step, in Bismarck's opinion[1], was to secure the home markets; and this was the object of the tariff of 1879. The case of Austria was different: she had been content to remain an agricultural country, and to receive her manufactured wares from England in exchange for raw products; but in the early seventies it became impossible to pursue this scheme, as her purchasing power was diminishing[2]. The extension of the American railway system had been carried so far that the development of the Great West had begun; the

[1] Lotz, *op. cit.* 166.
[2] Peez, *Die oesterreichische Handelspolitik*, in Leipsic *Schriften des Vereins für Socialpolitik*, XLIX. 176.

competition which has proved so prejudicial to English agriculturists was equally serious to Austrian dealers. They could no longer export on such terms as to purchase English manufactures at reasonable rates, and they determined to take the course of developing native manufactures, so that the country might be independent of the variations which arose from complications and developments in distant parts of the globe. They had found that economic inter-dependence played them false, and in 1878 they deliberately fell back on the independent organisation of national economic life.

This wide-spread reaction in the decade 1870—80 was brought about by felt practical requirements in different countries; and it was not by any means without intellectual justification. Frederick List had set an example in applying the historical method to economic questions; he laid great stress in his *National System of Political Economy* (1841) on the idea of development: he protested against the view of the dominant school of economists that the same principles could be advantageously applied in every country alike. He believed that when any nation had reached a high stage of progress Free Trade was the best policy for that particular country; but he also held that Free Trade failed to give the most favourable conditions for the economic development of countries which had the requisite capabilities but were for any reason backward. Even Mill had admitted that the temporary pro-tection of infant industries was excusable; List applied a similar doctrine on a much larger scale. He held up England as a model, and seems to have regarded her as the only country which had so successfully built up an economic system of her own[1], that she could wisely and safely run the risks of exposing her inhabitants to the full blast of foreign competition. He urged that cosmopolitanism would enable her to influence others unduly ; he insisted that the circumstances of England were exceptional, and the policy which was most advantageous to her was unfavourable to the development of all the resources of other countries ; it tended to keep them backward and poor.

In deliberately turning their backs during the Seventies upon the example set by England, the other countries were not definitely condemning her for the course she had adopted ; they were rather saying that it was one for which they were not themselves ripe. It appeared to be perfectly clear that so far as England was concerned there was a complete harmony between the cosmopolitan ideal and the national interest. The dominant factor on which the prosperity of her commerce depended was the manufacturing interest, and the English manufacturers had much to gain from Free Trade. During the eighteenth century they had obtained protection, but in the middle of the nineteenth they preferred to dispense with it. The Industrial Revolution had put them in such a position that protection could do little for them ; what they really wanted was the

---

[1] *National System of Political Economy*, 53.

fullest possible opportunity for disposing of their wares in any part of the world.

The fact that the manufacturers had changed sides from the Protectionist to the Free Trade camp had rendered the agitation which succeeded in 1846 possible; in England the industrial classes hold the key of the position, and their private interest as against foreign rivals differs according to the stage of their growth. A small boy will naturally desire a large handicap in the one or two events for which he enters in his school games. But if he grows up such a vigorous athlete that he can win any event by the full extent of his handicap, a large handicap ceases to be worth having. He does not desire protection. What he might really like would be—though it would scarcely be sportsmanlike—that there should be no restrictions of size or age, but that he might be free to enter for all the events, and to sweep off all the prizes. This removal of all limitations might suit one particular boy, but it would hardly be in the interest of all the boys at the same time. In the same way foreigners began to urge that Free Trade was not equally advantageous to all nations at the same time. They were inclined to think that England was pursuing a policy which suited her highly developed national life, and was trying, under the pretence of cosmopolitanism, to force it on other countries to which it was inapplicable. By 1880, the failure of Cobden's effort to induce other countries to adopt Free Trade had become conspicuous. In so far as they had tried it, they had come to the

conclusion that it did not suit them.   The futility of
this project, for laying a foundation of national interdependence on which a fabric of universal peace
might securely rest, had been thoroughly exposed.

iii.   *The restatement of the question.*

In 1880, when it became obvious that other
countries had decided against the adoption of Free
Trade, the whole question was set in a new light;
the prospects of cosmopolitan commercial intercourse
were changed.   The advocates of Free Trade had
been able to represent it as something that was
within the range of practical politics, and to take
for granted that, because their system was expedient
for the world as a whole, every part of the world
would be sure to adopt it sooner or later; it was a
mere question of time, and England was, as became
her, in advance of other countries.   The reversion to
protection showed that universal Free Trade could
not be realized within any brief period; and that the
example of England was not exercising a persuasive
influence.   The whole of the cosmopolitan enthusiasm
which lay behind the Free Trade movement was
damped; it could no longer be represented as a
simple remedy which would exorcise the angry
passions of rival nationalities.

It was of course true that the change of circumstances made no difference to the economic theory of
Free Trade.   The doctrine could perhaps be stated
with a little more precision, but that was all.   If
there were universal peace, and if every country had

reached its full economic development, the adoption of Free Trade would be beneficial to the world as a whole and especially to the consumers in every nation. As an abstract proposition no exception can be taken to the fundamental principle of Free Trade; so clearly is it true that it has no more practical value than any other truism. The methods which Cobden recommended of realising this improved condition had failed; and hence the question, for any men who were seriously in earnest about it, was to consider what other steps might offer a better prospect of securing the results he had hoped for. The abandonment of Cobden's methods had become perfectly compatible with a steadfast adherence to Cobden's ideal.

Even as regards England herself, the question was entirely altered. The prospective political effects of our course might be left out of account in any discussion of its wisdom; we were only called upon to view it as a matter of expediency, as it affected the prosperity of the United Kingdom. The constitutional results, which Cobden had had in view in the Corn Law agitation, had been gained; by 1880 the exclusive power of the landed aristocracy was broken and the English Government had come to rest on a democratic basis. The question of Free Trade had lost its moral significance; the issue was simplified by being limited to a discussion of the practical bearing of the new policy on the material well-being of the community. The fact that other nations had refused to follow in our track raised the suspicion in some minds that the line we had taken might not necessarily be the best for our own interests. Moreover, practical experience shewed that increased communication was not always beneficial ; the re-opening of the old route to the East by Suez had not been altogether to our advantage; there were signs that some of our industries were migrating, and that our monopoly of shipping was becoming less complete. Was the position of England really so exceptional, and her development so abnormal that the scheme which other countries had found prejudicial to themselves was really good for us ? These uneasy questionings found admirable expression in the speech which Lord Salisbury made at Hastings on 18th May, 1892 :—

"After all this little island lives as a trading island. We could not produce in foodstuffs enough to sustain the population that lives in this island, and it is only by the great industries which exist here and which find markets in foreign countries that we are able to maintain the vast population by which this island is inhabited.

"But a danger is growing up. Forty or so years ago everybody believed that Free Trade had conquered the world, and they prophesied that every nation would follow the example of England and give itself up to absolute Free Trade. The results are not exactly what they prophesied, but the more adverse the results were, the more the devoted prophets of Free Trade declared that all would come right at last; the worse the tariffs of foreign countries became, the more confident were the prophecies of an early victory. But we see now, after many years' experience that explain it, how foreign nations are raising one after another a wall, a brazen wall, of protection around their shores, which excludes us from their markets, and so far as they are concerned do their best to kill our trade. And this state of things does not get better. On the contrary, it constantly seems to get worse. Now, of course, if I utter a word with reference to Free Trade I shall be accused of being a protectionist, of a desire to over-throw Free Trade, and of all the other crimes which an ingenious imagination can attach to a commercial heterodoxy. But nevertheless I ask you to set yourselves free from all that merely vituperative doctrine, and to consider whether the true doctrine of Free Trade carries you as far as some of these gentlemen would wish you to go. Every true religion has its counterpart in inventions and legends and traditions which grow upon that religion. The Old Testament had its canonical books, and had also its Talmud and its Mishnah, the inventions of Rabbinical commentators. There are a Mish-nah and a Talmud constantly growing up. One of the difficulties we have to contend with is the strange and unreasonable doctrine which these Rabbis have imposed upon us. If we look abroad into the world we see it. In the office which I have the honour to hold I am obliged to see a great deal of it. We live in an age of a war of tariffs. Every nation is trying how it can, by agreement with its

neighbour, get the greatest possible protection for its
own industries, and at the same time the greatest
possible access to the markets of its neighbours.
This kind of negotiation is continually going on. It
has been going on for the last year and a half with
great activity. I want to point out to you that what
I observe is that while A. is very anxious to get a
favour of B., and B. is anxious to get a favour
of C., nobody cares two straws about getting
the commercial favour of Great Britain. What is
the reason of that? It is that in this great battle
Great Britain has deliberately stripped herself of the
armour and the weapons by which the battle has to
be fought. You cannot do business in this world of
evil and suffering on these terms. If you go to
market you must bring money with you. If you
fight you must fight with the weapons with which
those you have to contend against are fighting.
It is not easy for you to say, 'I am a Quaker,' 'I do
not fight at all, I have no weapon,' and to expect
that the people will pay the same regard to you and
be as anxious to obtain your good-will and to consult
your interests as they will do for the people who have
retained their armour and still hold their weapon.
The weapon with which they all fight is admission to
their own markets, that is to say, A. says to B., 'If
you will make your duties such that I can sell in
your market, I will make my duties such that you
can sell in my market.' But we begin by saying:
'We will levy no duties on anybody,' and we declare
that it would be contrary and disloyal to the glorious

and sacred doctrine of Free Trade to levy any duty on anybody for the sake of what we can get by it. It may be noble, but it is not business. On those terms you will get nothing, and I am sorry to have to tell you that you are practically getting nothing. The opinion of this country as stated by its authorised exponents has been opposed to what is called a retaliatory policy.

"We as the Government of the country at the time have laid it down for ourselves as a strict rule from which there is no departure, and we are bound not to alter the traditional policy of the country unless we are convinced that a large majority of the country is with us, because in these foreign affairs consistency of policy is beyond all things necessary.

"But though that is the case, still, if I may aspire to fill the office of a councillor to the public mind, I should ask you to form your own opinions without reference to traditions or denunciations—not to care two straws whether you are orthodox or not, but to form your opinions according to the dictates of common sense. I would impress upon you that if you intend, in this conflict of commercial treaties, to hold your own, you must be prepared, if need be, to inflict upon the nations which injure you the penalty which is in your hands, that of refusing them access to your markets. (A voice, 'Common Sense at last.') There is a reproach in that interruption but I have never said anything else. And there is a great difficulty. The Power we have most reason to complain of is the United States, and what we want the United States to furnish us with mostly are articles of food essential to the feeding of the people, and raw materials necessary to our manufactures, and we cannot exclude one or the other without serious injury to ourselves.

"Now I am not in the least prepared for the sake of wounding other nations to inflict any dangerous or serious wound upon ourselves. We must confine ourselves, at least for the present, to those subjects on which we should not suffer very much whether the importation continued or diminished, but what I complain about of the Rabbis of whom I have just spoken is that they confuse the vital point. They say that everything must be given to the consumer. Well, if the consumer is the man who maintains the industries of the country or is the people at large, I agree with the Rabbis. You cannot raise the price of food or of raw material, but there is an enormous mass of other articles of importation from other countries which are mere matters of luxurious consumption......But as one whose duty it is to say what he thinks to the people of this country, I am bound to say that our Rabbis have carried the matter too far. We must distinguish between consumer and consumer, and while jealously preserving the rights of a consumer who is coextensive with a whole industry or with the whole people of the country, we may fairly use our power over an importation which merely ministers to luxury, in order to maintain our own in this great commercial battle." This was at least an effective plea for the recognition of the fact that the question was assuming a very different aspect from that which it had presented to the public mind in the Forties and Fifties.

CHAPTER V.

IS ONE-SIDED FREE TRADE EXPEDIENT FOR ENGLAND?

So far we have been dealing with matter that is non-contentious—mere ancient history; but our hasty review of the rise of the Free Trade movement in the world, and of its decline since 1870, has brought us face to face with a burning question :—Is it worth while to reopen the controversy which seemed to have been decided in 1846 ? Is there even a *primâ facie* case for reconsidering the decision, or may we not regard it as a *chose jugée?* There is a very strong and very wise indisposition on the part of the English public against anything that seems to imply going back on what has been deliberately done by the nation. We have no written constitution; the whole stability of our system of government seems to depend on this habit of accepting an accomplished fact. Those who, in opposition, may be most strongly hostile to some proposed change generally make no attempt to reverse it when they get into power. They accept the inevitable and try to make the best of the scheme they have denounced. The obligation to take this line becomes infinitely stronger when there has been a definite appeal to the country, and the citizens have endorsed the action of Parliament; this was fully recognised by Disraeli in his Budget Speech in 1852[1], and by Lord Salisbury in 1892. The fact that, as we have seen, the decision was forced on by an apparently accidental conjuncture of circumstances does not greatly weigh with us; almost every important event in history can be represented, when we know about it in detail, as the outcome of some trivial incident. Nor need we be greatly influenced by the fact that the introduction of Free Trade has not accomplished all that was expected of it. The advocates of a change are always apt to be over-sanguine; and the fact that they miscalculated does not necessarily shew that the course on which we entered nearly sixty years ago was unwise. Granted that Free Trade, as we adopted it, has not proved to be a stepping-stone to universal Free Trade, but that we have been thrown back on a scheme of one-sided

---

[1] "We wished, after the event of the last general election, understanding as we did from the result of that election that the principle of unrestricted competition was entirely and finally adopted as the principle of our commercial code—we wished to consider our financial system in relation to our commercial system—to see whether they could not be brought more in harmony together, and whether in bringing them more in harmony together, we might not...lay the foundations of a system which should not only in future be more beneficial, but which should enlist in its favour the sympathies of all classes." 3 *Hansard*, cxxiii. 838.

Free Trade[1], may we not have reason to be satisfied
with it, as sound in principle, and successful in
practice? Hence we are forced to consider how far
insular Free Trade is conducive to English prosperity.
Just as we discussed the good and bad of the
Mercantile System, as it existed during the second
quarter of the nineteenth century, so we may examine
how far, during the twenty-five years with which it
closed, one-sided Free Trade has been really beneficial
in promoting the national prosperity of England.
Statisticians are content to get at the history of the
recent past as accurately as possible, but we are
rather concerned to examine the stability of our
present conditions, and to ask how far they portend
a continuance of national prosperity.

i.   *The Extension of Trade and Industry.*

There can be no doubt that, when tried by any
ordinary criterion, there has been an enormous growth
of national industry and commerce since Free Trade
was adopted in 1846.   We may take the method of
measurement which Sir Robert Peel employed in
shewing that the tentative movement in the direction
of one-sided Free Trade, on which England entered
in 1842, had been successful[2], and enquire as to the
value of our exports.   They may be regarded as probably indicating that the productive power is vigorous,

---

[1] This term was used by Disraeli in 1852.   "I look," he said,
"on one-sided free-trade as an obsolete opinion."   3 *Hansard*,
cxxiii. 858.

[2] 27 Jan. 1846.   3 *Hansard*, lxxxiii. 277.

and as certainly shewing that the country has a
large amount of purchasing power with which it can
procure commodities, or make investments in other
lands.

The figures, in millions, as given in the recent
Board of Trade Report[1] are as follows :

1840	£51,000,000.
1850	£71,000,000.
1860	£135,000,000.
1870	£199,000,000.
1880	£223,000,000.
1890	£263,000,000.
1900	£282,000,000.

The year 1840 shows the condition of English
trade, after the chief mechanical changes which were
comprised in the Industrial Revolution had been
introduced, but before Peel's changes in the tariff
began in 1842. The growth which has gone on since
that time has doubtless been partly influenced by the
development of steam navigation and other causes ;
but it is impossible to tell what allowance ought to
be made for these influences ; and we can certainly
say that under the scheme which England adopted in
1846 there has been an enormous growth. At the
same time, it is clear that the rate of progress has not
been maintained in the last decades. We may take
1850 as the year when the influence of the new policy
began to be felt; the value of the exports had increased

---

[1] *Memoranda, Statistical Tables and Charts with reference to
British and Foreign Trade and Industrial Conditions*, 1903.

ninety per cent.—from £71,000,000 to £135,000,000—
before the decade was out. During the next decade the
increase was forty-seven per cent.; from 1870 to 1880
the rate of increase fell to twelve per cent.; and
though in the following decade it rose to nearly
eighteen per cent., in the last decade of last century
it dropped to seven per cent. This diminishing rate
of increase should not be overlooked ; though it may
be the opinion of the ordinary man, who is a little
suspicious that statistics lend themselves to the
subtlest forms of special pleading, that so long as
progress continues, even though it be at a diminished
rate, we need not greatly concern ourselves about
the principles we have adopted.

ii. *Is this development wholesome?*

The magnitude of the development of our export
trade is not, however, in itself conclusive ; it is after
all only one test of the economic condition of the
country—though a very useful test. We may remember that, as we had occasion to notice, the
Mercantile System was admirably successful when
tried by the criterion which its founders would have
applied ; it had built up the maritime power of
England, and afforded an enormous revenue for naval
and military purposes. At the same time, when
viewed in other aspects, it was condemned. We are
therefore called upon to look a little more closely at
the scheme of insular Free Trade, and to ask whether
this great development is really wholesome ? We are
less concerned with the rapid growth than with the

stability of our national wealth.   Can the progress
which has been taking place go on indefinitely with
greater and greater benefit to the nation as a whole?

(a)   There are two points that deserve consideration; for one thing insular Free Trade, like
Mercantilism in its last days[1], is a one-sided system.
It has apparently benefited commerce and manufactures, but one great side of national economic life
has suffered.   Since agriculture has not flourished
under this scheme of policy, we are forced to recognise
that this great economic development has been one-
sided ; the country has not prospered all round.   In
this respect the progress of recent years is less
satisfactory than the real, but slow, advance which
occurred under the Mercantile System in the
eighteenth century.   That was an all-round development, in which interests of every sort participated;
commerce, manufactures, and land were all cared for,
stimulated, and benefited[2]; but in the last quarter of
the nineteenth century the loss in one great field of
national enterprise and the industries which are
connected with it[3], must be set against the gain in
others, before the general effect on the community as
a whole can be satisfactorily estimated.

Till 1874 it could hardly have been said that
agriculture had failed to share in the general prosperity of the Free Trade era; it appeared as if

[1] During the period from 1815 to 1845.   See above, p. 58.

[2] See above, p. 29.

[3] See Mr Druce's evidence (9140) in *Report of Commission on
Depression of Trade* (1886), xxiii. 65.

Cobden's anticipations, as regards the rural districts, had been completely justified, for there had been no ruinous fall in the price of agricultural products. To this result several unforeseen influences had contributed; the Crimean War shut up the sources of Russian supply, and prevented Russian competition from coming into play; while the American Civil War in 1861 delayed the development, by railways, and labour saving machinery, of the wheat-growing regions of the West. Since 1875 the forebodings of the agriculturists—which Cobden dismissed with scorn—have been realised. The state of the case has been excellently summarised by Mr Inglis Palgrave—one of the few living economists whose work is of such a standard that he has been elected a Fellow of the Royal Society. As a banker of established reputation who was for many years editor of the *Economist* and subsequently of *The Dictionary of Political Economy* his knowledge is very wide, and his calculations deserve the most careful consideration. He estimates that during the twenty years from 1883 the landed interest, especially the landlords and tenant-farmers, lost a sum which approximates to £800,000,000[1]. If the prices of 1874 had been kept up they would have been richer at the present time by nearly the amount of the National Debt. This is a considerable amount for any class to lose, and it is not to be neglected in discussing the wealth of the community as a whole.

[1] *Economic Condition of the Country* in *National Review*, Nov. 1903, p. 402.

The nation can perhaps afford to lose it, and the gain from other sources may serve to recoup this loss and more; but at least it may be said that the great development of prosperity to which the figures of our export trade testify has been one-sided, since an important factor in the economic life of the country has suffered so much.

(b) Again, it must be remembered that this great development has been, not only one-sided, but artificial. Protective legislation is most easily justified economically when it aims at fostering some industry for which the country really possesses great advantages, and thus stimulates development along natural lines. The Mercantile System had this character to a very large extent in the eighteenth century; but the advocates of Free Trade desired a more careful reliance on the guidance of nature. Adam Smith was inclined to condemn any departure from the natural progress of opulence. He held that the legislator ought to take account of the resources of the country, the climate, soil, geographical position and harbours, and build up the economic fabric on this basis. Cobden was even more decided in his view that the very meaning of Free Trade was that it gave free play to nature, and afforded every nation the opportunity of taking advantage of the natural gifts bestowed on different parts of the world. He was anxious that politicians should not interfere with prices, or the natural development be distorted by the demands of particular classes, and the jealousies of different countries. But the lines of our recent development have ceased to be determined by natural conditions; the direction of our industry is controlled, not by our own politicians, but by the statesmen of other countries. The Englishman is no longer master in his own house, but pursues the occupations that his neighbours assign him. We are forced to relinquish certain manufactures for which our country is well adapted, because of the encouragements which foreigners give to their own industries, and the discouragements they place on the importation of our wares. We are compelled to devote ourselves, not to those things which we are naturally fitted to do best, but to those trades which they are inclined to leave to us, for the present at all events. It may be, as is alleged, that these are very profitable industries and exceedingly well worth carrying on; but the development is not natural. In defending our present scheme, the fundamental position of those who advocated Free Trade in the eighteenth century, and of those who carried it through in the nineteenth, must be abandoned. The Cobden Club no longer contend for a natural distribution of industry, but for the maintenance of an unnatural distribution which pays. In 1886, Mr Medley wrote in one of their publications, "that very powerful arguments can be adduced in favour of the view I hold, which is that considering where we stand now, universal Free Trade, though it would incalculably benefit the world at large, might not be that unmixed national blessing to us which it is presumed by many it would be.... If universal Free Trade prevailed, it is certain that articles would be manufactured where production could be most cheaply carried on. If so, we have to ask ourselves, Is Great Britain the cheapest place for the production of iron and steel, or of ships, or of cotton goods, or of machinery?...These considerations are quite enough to cast a doubt on the assumption that protective tariffs prevent us from doing a larger trade than we otherwise should do, and to make us think that universal Free Trade might not maintain us in the commanding position we now hold[1]." As an illustration it may suffice to say that the confectionery trade seems to have been aided by the foreign sugar bounties[2], and our ship-building by the dumping of foreign steel and iron[3]. To whatever extent this is true, the form which our industry takes at present is artificial, and the official advocates of insular Free Trade recognise that this is the case. As a German admirer of our present system put it when defending 'chronic dumping,'— " Whether the greater cheapness comes artificially or naturally does not matter[4]." This may be so, if we do not wish to look behind quotations of prices at the present hour; but the natural distribution of industry throughout the world is of vast importance, if we are trying to take the stability of industrial prosperity in each country, and the preservation of friendly relations between different communities, into account.

[1] G. W. Medley, *Pamphlets and Addresses*, 184–8.
[2] Sir V. H. P. Caillard, *Imperial Fiscal Reform*, 85.
[3] W. J. Ashley, *Tariff Problem*, 112.
[4] H. Dietzel, *British Association*, F., *Standard*, 20 Aug., 1904.

iii. *The probable Effects on National Resources,*
personal and physical.

Even though there may be a general consensus of opinion as to the character of an existing system, there is not likely to be much unanimity in the anticipations which different people may indulge as to the probable effects of continued development along these lines. Modern society is complex, and the phenomena with which we are concerned are in a constant state of flux ; observation is difficult, and it is not easy to discern the trend of affairs with any precision. The slow and cumulative action of such an influence as a national economic policy is particularly difficult to trace or to gauge. But there are two points which we may endeavour to consider. By common consent[1] the great resources of any country—on which its material prosperity depends —are twofold ; on the one hand there is the population, and on the other the physical possessions which may be included in the term land. These are the two factors which are essential to the maintenance and progress of the material welfare of any country. We may try to see how each of them is likely to be affected by insular Free Trade.

(*a*) The rapid growth of manufacturing, with no corresponding agricultural progress, might be expected to have serious results upon the population.   There

---

[1] Compare Hobbes, *English Works*, iii. 232, and Locke, *Civil Government*, in *Works*, iv. §§ 37, 40, 42.

is not indeed any likelihood, as there might have
been in earlier days, that the numbers would decline
for want of sufficient produce to maintain them;
there are such facilities for purchasing corn in foreign
parts that an ample supply of cheap food has been
forthcoming; while this is the case there is every
prospect that the numbers of the population will be
at least maintained. Cheap food gives the opportunity of an increase of population; according to the
best established of all the generalisations of Economic
Science there is a tendency for population to increase
up to the limit set by the means of subsistence. The
researches of Malthus went to shew that cheap food
is in itself a doubtful benefit to a community—the
mere rendering of the necessaries of life less expensive
may give rise to a redundant population. The cases
of the negro population in tropical countries, and of
the natives of southern Italy and of Ireland, have
all been stock illustrations of the evils which may
accrue from the cheapness of food in a country where
there is either the lack of will or the lack of opportunity to obtain work. This state of affairs has not
been unknown in England. In the time of Elizabeth,
and again at the era of the Revolution, there seem
to have been a large number of idle members of the
body politic, and the difficulty of planting and fostering industries so that they might be absorbed in the
active life of the community, was a problem with
which public authorities and philanthropists alike
were always endeavouring to deal. Under modern
conditions there is a danger of the recurrence of the

same evil[1]. The mechanical improvements of the
last hundred years have given an increased means of
purchasing food, but have in some ways curtailed
opportunities for employment, especially in rural
districts. In these circumstances the existence of a
"submerged population" in our towns, and of serious
overcrowding need not be a matter of surprise ; it is
exactly what we might expect to happen, and what is
likely to continue under the existing conditions of
cheap food and inconstant employment.

There is also a considerable probability that when
the population is redundant, there will be a deterioration in its quality, both physical and moral. It has
been a widely spread opinion for generations that the
portion of the population which had most stamina
was that which was bred and reared in the rural
districts, and that the increase of an urban, relatively
to a rural, population was in many ways undesirable.
According to Mr J. R. Macculloch this was an evil
which was closely connected with the growth of
factory industry, and it was one for which he saw no
remedy[2]. He underrated the force of the corrections
which have been introduced through the association
of skilled workers ; but it would be difficult to shew
that the tendency he noted has been inoperative.

[1] Cobden's scheme of providing increased employment without
lowering the price of food would, if it had been practicable, have
done nothing to encourage the growth of a redundant population.
Insular Free Trade as it has worked out with supplies of cheap
food, and entire carelessness about the matter of employment,
affords no safeguard against "boy and girl marriages," among
populations who obtain work casually.

[2] *Treatises and Essays* (1859), 454.

The trend of migration from rural districts to towns has certainly gone on much more rapidly than he expected, for he did not anticipate that agriculture would be exposed to disastrous competition. There are hardly sufficient accurate data available to make it perfectly clear whether the alleged deterioration of the national physique is well founded, and it would probably be impossible to get any evidence as to changes in rural stamina ; but for all that, the tendency may exist even if the numerous activities, both municipal and philanthropic, for improving the conditions in which the poor live and work, have succeeded in counteracting it altogether. It is easy to propound heroic remedies for overcrowding, and to insist that municipalities should provide adequate house accommodation ; it is still simpler to blame owners or landowners for the existing state of affairs; but it is difficult to be sure that the one-sided development of our economic life has not tended to aggravate the evil.

(b) There is far less difficulty in getting at the facts in regard to the other factor of continued national prosperity, and in seeing how it is faring with our physical resources.

So far as the surface of the land is concerned there can be no doubt that the acreage which is under tillage has been greatly reduced during the last thirty years. The area of corn crops in the United Kingdom has shrunk more and more, from 11,543,777 acres in 1871–5 to 8,392,863 acres in 1903[1]. This does not

[1] *Agricultural Returns* (Board of Agriculture and Fisheries), 1903, p. 44.

mean that pasture farming has become more profitable, and that the tenants find it wiser to devote
their attention to stock breeding rather than to
husbandry. The grass counties have suffered from
a fall in the value of stock, just as the arable counties
have from a fall in the value of wheat—though not to
the same extent as yet. Nor is it true to suppose
that agricultural land is a mere natural gift; an
English farm is a highly complicated product of
civilisation, and if it is disused for a time, or badly
used, it deteriorates in every way. The machinery
becomes valueless, the buildings go out of repair,
and the land itself becomes foul. Land lying idle, or
land badly cultivated, is the outward symbol of the
ruin that has overtaken many districts. The whole
industry in all its branches has been very severely hit,
and the loss has affected every class connected with
the agricultural interest. The landlords are the
class who had most to lose, and their loss, in the
capitalised value of their greatly reduced rentals, has
been enormous. There is a general impression that
this is merely the private concern of a class, and does
not really imply any injury to the community; but
it is a mistake to suppose that English landlords are
mere rent receivers, who obtain an unearned income
by merely allowing other people to work their land;
they actively co-operate with their capital in the maintenance of farming buildings and the improvement of
the soil. The impoverishment of the landlord class
means that there is much less capital available for
working the land of the country effectively, and that

this great national asset is not being utilised to its fullest extent.

The impoverishment of the landlords is having another result, in the increase of absenteeism. Men can no longer afford to reside on their estates, and are forced to let their country houses to wealthy city men who occupy them as occasional holiday resorts. The social evils of such absenteeism do not concern us, when we are applying ourselves to a strictly economic question; but it is worth while to remember that in earlier days severe measures were taken by the Crown to check the growing non-residence by the country gentry. The economic effects of absenteeism on village life may be very serious, in doing away with a considerable local demand for produce of many kinds, and cutting down the opportunities of employment. It is particularly unfortunate, too, that at a time when there seems to be the need to introduce more co-operation and organisation in rural districts, those who are from their position most competent to take a lead in the matter should be losing touch with local interests and requirements. In the eighteenth century, when agriculture was remunerative, there were many spirited proprietors who set an example by introducing improvements, and inducing their tenants and neighbours to adopt them. It is not the least serious feature of the present agricultural distress that so many proprietors are not only without the capital, but unable to retain the position which is necessary for a pioneer.

The loss as regards the labouring class has been
of a different kind ; many of them have been forced
to go to towns, and to emigrate, and some have doubtless become more prosperous personally in their new
surroundings than they would have done in the old
conditions ; though it is not likely that the change
has been for the better in all cases. The diminution
of employment in rural districts, with the overcrowding
of the towns, is an evil, even if each generation of
immigrants succeeds in keeping a relatively high level
in their new surroundings. The reduction of the
demand for rural labour has had its natural effect in
a diminution of supply ; and a consequent rise in the
rate of rural wages. This does not appear to have
been accompanied by any obvious increase in efficiency,
so that there is, generally speaking, a considerably
higher expense for labour in connection with agricultural production than was formerly the case.

Under these circumstances it cannot be said that
the position of the tenant-farmer is very satisfactory.
He has not to pay nearly such a high rent as fell on
him in 1874, but the landlord is less able to co-
operate with him in improvement. Prices have
fallen, but his labour bill is far higher than it was.
Viewing the matter as a whole we may say that
under influence of insular Free Trade there has not
only been an enormous loss, but the industry has
been so far disorganised that there is great difficulty
in facing the new conditions and trying to make the
best of them.

Besides its agriculture, another very valuable

national asset is the mineral wealth of the country ; and this is necessarily being exhausted. The art of tillage consists in getting a large amount of produce every year without exhausting the soil, but the labour of the miner is extractive, and no known art can replace what he takes away. This is sufficiently obvious, and the precise rate of exhaustion is not a point on which it is necessary to spend much time. In so far as our present industrial prosperity depends on native supplies of coal and iron, it rests on an insecure foundation, since these supplies are being used up with greater or less rapidity[1]. Attention was first directed to the seriousness of the problem in 1865 by the late Professor W. Stanley Jevons[2]. In 1891 I heard a discussion of the subject at the British Association Meeting at Cardiff, when Mr T. Forster Brown stated that the maximum output would probably be reached in twenty-five years, and continue for another twenty-five years ; and that after that period another element in the commercial position of the nation—a greatly enhanced cost of fuel—would begin to be felt[3]. England has already had experience of the effects of a deficient supply of fuel ; in the seventeenth and eighteenth centuries the supply of wood for fuel was running low, and a serious stagnation resulted in some of the staple

[1] W. J. Ashley, *The Tariff Problem*, 100.

[2] " To allow commerce to proceed until the source of civilisation is weakened and overturned is like killing the goose to get the golden egg." *The Coal Question*, 345.

[3] *British Association Report*, 1891, p. 736.

industries. The revenue shewed no elasticity, and
there was great difficulty in meeting the annual
charges on our debt. It was only by the series of
inventions and discoveries, which rendered it possible
to substitute coal for wood in the smelting and
working of iron, that England was relieved from this
depressing influence and enabled to make the
enormous advance she did. It is needless to point
out that in the present day dear fuel would affect not
only the hardware trades, but all the various industries, textile and others, in which steam power is
employed. This national asset is of supreme importance, and while it would be absurd to contend that
our mineral treasures should be hoarded and not used,
it is worth consideration whether we are shewing the
sort of good management which would be exercised by
a private owner, and forming investments which adequately represent in the national capital account the
value of the extracted coal[1].

iv. *The Balance of Loss and Gain.*

This brief survey of the condition of the country,
after half-a-century of one-sided Free Trade, seems to
shew that the *primâ facie* case for reconsidering the

---

[1] "The energy of fuel is derived from the sun's rays; coal being
the store which nature has laid up as a species of capital for us,
while wood is our precarious yearly income. We are thus at
present (1873) very much in the position of a young heir, who has
only recently come into his estates, and who, not content with the
income, is rapidly squandering his realized property." Balfour
Stewart, *Conservation of Energy*, 144.

decision taken in 1846 is exceedingly strong. A great development has occurred, but it has been so one-sided and artificial that it can hardly be regarded as healthy; the opinion of Napoleon and his contemporaries as to the instability of the British Colossus[1], is much more nearly true under the *régime* of insular Free Trade than under the Mercantile System of the eighteenth century. The alleged deterioration of our population and the waste and exhaustion of our physical resources are serious symptoms; it is difficult to share the complacent optimism which finds expression in many quarters. In spite of the growth of our export trade, the doubt may well arise whether our industrial prosperity is sound, and whether it can be developed with advantage farther and farther along the existing lines.

The doubt becomes more serious when we compare the recent industrial development of this country with that of some of her neighbours. England is not by any means the only country that has enjoyed a growing trade during the last thirty years; Germany and America have also prospered in an extraordinary fashion, and while the rate of progress in England is decreasing, the United States are developing their trade with increasing rapidity. The exports from England have grown absolutely, but relatively to the advance made by other countries England has fallen behind in the race.

The popular explanation of this state of affairs is not altogether reassuring. It is said that England

[1] Cunningham, *Growth of English Industry*, II. 677.

is an older country; that America is young; that
therefore the rate of progress in the United States is
necessarily greater, and that we should be perfectly
satisfied so long as we continue to grow at all.   But
after all the terms 'young' and 'old' are not very
illuminating; the distinction which is important
economically does not lie in the age of a state in
years, but in the character of its productions.   During
the eighteenth century England was a country which
exported corn; this was a commodity the amount of
which could not generally speaking be increased,
except at an increased rate of expense.   Trade which
is founded on such products cannot be expanded
indefinitely, and an 'old' and high civilisation cannot
expect to carry on such commerce.   But with manufactures the case is different; an increased amount
can be obtained at a diminishing cost of production,
except in so far as it is counterbalanced by an increasing dearness of food, of fuel, or of materials.
Just because England was already manufacturing on
a large scale, she had an enormous advantage for
increasing her lead; the same principle must be
borne in mind with regard to our shipping.   According
to Sir A. Swettenham, "the Singapore region has
been developing very largely in the last twenty years,
and there has been an enormous increase of trade all
round," but in looking at statistics he thinks it will
be found that "we were the very first in the field, and
we have had all our agencies established, and we had
a very large amount of shipping in our possession;
and other things being equal, certainly ought to have

developed at the same rate as others, if not faster, because being on the spot, and having everything going like clockwork, it would have been easier for us to have increased our trade than for others who were not on the spot. What we find is that the foreigners, or certain foreigners, notably the Germans and Japanese, have increased their trade very much more rapidly and very much more efficiently than we have done[1]." England could apparently add to her production more cheaply than other countries working on a smaller scale could add to theirs. When we get rid of the delusive analogies about 'young' and 'old,' we see that, considering the character of English industry, the trade founded upon it can hardly be said to have been really prosperous, since we have lost the lead we once enjoyed in the steel and iron trades, while neither woollen[2] nor cotton[3] can be regarded as flourishing industries.

The view of English economic life, which is accepted by some advocates of one-sided Free Trade, is to my mind a further reason for reconsidering the decision which was taken in 1846. It is a counsel of despair. We are told that we are merely helpless—and that anything we may attempt will only make matters worse. We have a large redundant population—

[1] *Report of Select Committee on Steamship Subsidies*, 1902, IX. 312.

[2] *Minority Report of Royal Commission on Depression of Trade*, 1886, XXIII. 554 and 560.

[3] W. A. Abram, *Prospective Decline of Lancashire* in *Blackwood*, July, 1892, Vol. 152, and Helm in *Quarterly Journal of Economics*, XVII. May, 1903.

13,000,000 of people on the margin of starvation—
therefore we must have cheap food at all hazards,
even at the risk of perpetuating and increasing this
class. Our agriculture has decayed, but we cannot
help it ; our coal is being exhausted, but there is
nothing to be done. There was a time when the
principle of *laissez-faire* was put forward as stating
a condition which would enable the enterprising man
to use his opportunities for his own greatest advantage
and that of the nation ; it has become a mere sub-
terfuge under which carelessness of national interests
and indifference to national duty may cloak themselves. This patient acquiescence in a policy of
drift is a serious symptom of decadence, but it is not
so deep-seated as to be ineradicable. We have got
rid of it in regard to the conditions of labour; the
whole system of the factory and mines Acts, and of
factory and workshop inspection, is the expression of
a definite opinion that regulation and organisation
are desirable. We have got rid of *laissez-faire* in
many matters connected with the conditions of life—
the sanitary state of towns, and the training of
children ; these are matters which ought to be
attended to, and not left to drift. We have got rid of
laissez-faire in many matters of business, in the
control exercised over internal communication by
railways, and in the subsidising of shipping companies. The policy of drift is only maintained in the
sphere where it is most disastrous to the dignity
and reputation of the nation—our commercial intercourse with other lands and with our own colonies.

We cannot hope to win, or to retain, the respect of our neighbours, or the attachment of English peoples beyond the sea, unless we abandon this decadent lassitude and make an effort to face the difficulties that beset us. They are great, but they will only be fatal if we allow ourselves to be supine. Before all things it is necessary that we should carefully reconsider our position, and see if there is any way in which it can be improved.

CHAPTER VI.

EXPERT OPINION.

MANY English citizens who are inclined to think that there is a *primâ facie* case for reconsidering the relative advantages of pursuing the system of one-sided Free Trade and of making some new departure, may yet feel doubtful of their own competence to come to a right decision, either one way or the other. The case is very complex, and there is a mass of plausible statements which it seems impossible for anyone but an expert to sift, so as to form a trustworthy judgment. Unfortunately, public confidence in economic experts has been somewhat shaken. During the first half of the nineteenth century they were ready to offer their guidance with considerable confidence, and educated men were on the whole disposed to accept it. These days have passed away, and there is a disposition in many quarters to resent the very appearance of academic pretensions to deliver an authoritative opinion on public affairs[1]. Still, the

[1] *Times*, 15 Aug. 1903.

plain man, who sneers at "scholars who be hoodwinkt and brought up within the walks of a Colledge[1]," may be distrustful of his own judgment and inclined to think that deference should be paid to Economic Science after all. But this science does not pose as a master that demands deference; it offers itself as a servant, who is ready to give such help as is asked for. As a servant, it is invaluable in assisting the judgment and suggesting a course that may be tried; but a good servant may sometimes prove to be a very bad master. Despite its many merits, there are good reasons for refusing to look to Economic Science as an authority which can lay down the law about any practical question and settle it offhand. Beginners in the study of Economics are impressed by the acute analysis and forcible reasoning which serve to lay bare the inner grounds of complex human action. They feel the glamour of a study which brings order and system into the social chaos, and they can hardly help being enthusiastic advocates of the claims of the science to speak with authority. It seems to throw such searching light, that the conclusions reached appear to have demonstrative certainty. The more advanced student, however, is not unlikely to feel some hesitation as to whether these pretensions to speak authoritatively are really well founded; he will have learned that Economics is better fitted to play the part of the solicitors who get up the case on each side, than that of a Court of Appeal delivering judgment.

[1] Fenton, *Treatise of Usury*.

i.   *Economic Science as a Master.*

Economic Science owes much of its attractiveness
to the manner in which it introduces clearness and
accuracy into the rough and ready discussions of
ordinary life.   The terms which are bandied about
in popular discourse can be taken up and treated
with precision ; and the confusions of thought, which
lurk under vague language, can be exposed by careful
analysis[1].   But in grasping at this advantage—and
it is a great advantage—we run the risk of losing
touch with actual affairs ; we need to be on our
guard against habituating ourselves to think and
argue in an unreal world of notions, that are not
quite apposite to the conditions of actual life.
Adam Smith's main achievement lay in his success
in analysing the notion of Value-in-Exchange, and
making it, as newly explained, the basis of his
whole system of Natural Liberty.   Since his time
there has been an immense advance in the accurate
definition of terms ; these are the great landmarks
of the progress of Economic Science in its more
formal aspects, and they serve as instruments for the
better description and classification of complicated
phenomena.   But the tyro in Economics is in danger
of assuming too hastily that the phenomena which
bear some name in actual life correspond to the term

---

[1] On the importance of this formal side of Economic Study see
Cunningham, *A Plea for Pure Theory* in *The Economic Review*, II.
30.   It is a necessary element in the lucid discussion of economic
phenomena.

as he has become accustomed to define it. It was a very great achievement on the part of Ricardo to give us a doctrine of 'rent' as an economic conception, but the actual rents of everyday life are of many kinds and do not all correspond at all closely to the scientific definition. The prejudice against English landlords—as if they were mere receivers of 'economic rent,' and as if their interests were quite distinct from those of the tenant-farmer[1] and the labourer— has been due, in no small degree, to a misconception on this point. The payments made to a landlord under the name of rent include the profit on the capital he has sunk in the land, as well as a payment for the advantages which his land possesses over other land which supplies the same markets. The economic term is perfectly clear, but it is a mistake to assume that it applies precisely to the actual phenomena of English agriculture.

There is a danger of the same sort of error in regard to economic forces. The science, rightly and necessarily, separates out the desire of material wealth as an important factor in human life ; by isolating it and following out its probable effects systematically[2] we get the explanation of a large part of human affairs. Only persons of a cynical temperament would be prepared to assert that this account of human life was exhaustive, and that no such motives as political ambition or family feeling were ever operative as

[1] On the convergence of these interests see J. S. Nicholson, *Tenants' Gain not Landlords' Loss.*

[2] Buckle, *History of Civilisation,* II. 442.

modifying influences. The tyro is apt to use language which conveys the mistaken impression that such cynicism is an established scientific axiom[1]. The principles of Economic Science give us a clear statement of the manner in which one great force tends to act, but we need to examine the conditions of place and time before we can be sure that conflicting tendencies may be neglected and that this force is operating freely in any society. Economic principles are very clear, but they are not to be altogether trusted as representing the play of forces in actual life.

To put it in another way. Before any science can be accepted as an authority, which is entitled to lay down the law for our guidance, two things are necessary ; the student must not only have clear notions, he must also be sure of his facts. The economist's ideas may be perfectly clear, but the competent student knows that he cannot be sure of his facts with the confidence which physicists or chemists are entitled to feel. With the growth and development of society, with the advances of invention and the progress of organisation, the subject-matter of Economic Science is constantly changing ; there is continual flux, and, on the whole, progress ; nothing remains stationary. The phenomena, with which the

[1] Cobden appears to have been under the mistaken impression that this was the case, and allowed himself to take a very low view of his opponents. He felt that the advantages of Free Trade were clear ; and he was apt to account for any opposition to his views by asserting that his opponents were swayed by merely interested motives.

chemist deals are different in kind; the same conditions can be produced in a laboratory, the same substance may be analysed over again, the results can be confirmed or corrected. There is the opportunity for recurring observation, and for obtaining well-established data in regard to phenomena that continue unaltered during the whole period of human existence on the globe. In Economics, which studies the phenomena that arise through the changing desires and powers of men in utilising physical conditions, there cannot be any similarly solid basis of knowledge. We cannot get results that hold good for the whole period of the earth's history, or of human life; the subject-matter has always been changing more or less; and in the age in which we live it is changing with extraordinary rapidity. In Mill's time it was possible to separate the history of the globe into long ages of custom—dark and scientifically inexplicable[1]—and the age of competition which was coming into being in all progressive countries. But we now see that the conceptions which are most appropriate to one progressive country are inappropriate to others; the same analysis does not apply to those that are most closely akin. The economic life of the two branches of the Anglo-Saxon race is so distinct that the terms and analysis which are most convenient in dealing with the one

[1] Modern Economic Science does not limit its range in this manner, but endeavours to take account of economic phenomena in communities of every type. K. Bücher, *Entstehung der Volkswirthschaft*, 8. Cunningham, *Plea for Pure Theory* in *Economic Review*, II. 27.

are inadequate to a proper comprehension of the other. Professor Jenks rightly observes that "the 'normal price' of economists has been based upon cost of production under a system of competition among small capitalists"; and that under the conditions in the sugar industry in America this conception does not apply. "There is no normal level of competitive price based on the cost of production[1]." The ordinary economic analysis of English industry is inapplicable to American developments. Fifty years ago it seemed possible to take for granted that the conditions which prevailed in England gave us a type which would continue here, and to which other countries would gradually conform. The classical school of economists were always inclined to assume that the phenomena of their own time were permanent, and to generalise too hastily from the special conditions with which they were themselves familiar. They were as a consequence somewhat ready to assume the attitude of a master, and to lay down the law to public men as to the course which ought to be pursued. On purely *doctrinaire* grounds, and in opposition to the opinion of practical men in all parts of the country, they did away with the system of technical training by apprenticeship without attempting to provide a substitute; they were satisfied that it would suffice to let every boy learn his business as best he could. We have, as a nation, paid a heavy price for accepting such expert guidance. In a similar fashion,

[1] *The Trust Problem* (1901), 141, 142.

and in the same *doctrinaire* spirit, the principles of
colonial preference and of the Navigation Acts were
abandoned in the Forties. Vigorous protests against
the repealing measure were made at the time. "It
was," as Lord Winchelsea said, "carrying out the
principle of Free Trade with the most utter reckless-
ness that had ever characterised a deliberative or
national assembly. We had practical experience of
our Navigation Laws. He defied any man to deny
that under these laws England had risen above all
other nations in the world to a just and proud
dominion over the seas. And they were now to
abandon this dominion for the adoption of a mere
speculative measure of this Free Trade character[1]."
The Government were able to carry their measure,
but recent experience makes it clear that the anticipations of their critics were not merely wild[2].

There has been a great advance in every department of Economic Science during the last fifty years;
and one of the most noticeable marks of progress is

[1] 12th June, 1849. 3 *Hansard*, CVI. 20.

[2] Compare Sir R. Giffen's evidence before the *Select Committee
on Steamship Subsidies*. "What I have said is, in fact, a proposal
to revive, in part, the Navigation Laws, which were abolished, amid
great applause, half-a-century ago; and the excuse is the change of
circumstances. It has been assumed in some quarters that our
experience of the trade of the country since the repealing of the
Navigation Laws has proved Adam Smith's apprehensions to be
groundless—that we can trust to Free Trade in this matter; but
whether we could do so or not if there were no unfair competition,
what we have to face is really a hostile attack on a vital industry
of the country in time of peace, carried on, directly or indirectly,
not by ordinary competitors but by foreign governments." *Reports*
(1902), IX. 396.

that economists are more profoundly conscious of
the limitations of their science. The principles of
economic science are generalisations which are more
or less widely true ; they give us a basis for saying
what is probable under certain circumstances. But
they never can supply statements that are universally
valid in the world of fact ; and therefore they never
can tell us what *must* happen. The economic 'must'
is a survival from an earlier phase of the science
which has been superseded ; it belongs to the age of
the doctrines of the 'wages fund,' and of the 'last
hour.' The expert, who at the present day asserts
that imports 'must' be paid for by exports, or that
goods 'must' be paid for with goods is taking a tone
he has no right to adopt. It is perfectly clear that
on the whole and generally a purchaser 'must' pay
for the goods he receives, or shopkeepers will not
continue to supply him ; as an abstract proposition
he 'must' pay for what he receives. There are
probably a large number of places in which the statement that a man 'must' live within his income is
true in fact. It may even be generally true, but it is
not true universally ; there are places in which and
expedients by which it is possible for a man to live
beyond his income for a long series of years. The
public are not ready now-a-days to bow to the *ipse
dixit* of the expert, and competent students no longer
pose as authorities who can lay down the law for all
times and places.

ii. *Economic Science as a Servant.*

While Economic Science cannot lay down general principles which apply to all communities alike in all parts of the world, it can be of great assistance (*a*) in criticising a course that has been pursued, or (*b*) in devising the means which may be adopted in any given place and time for securing some particular result.

(*a*) From the time of Lord Burleigh onwards, for a period of two hundred years, the English nation knew very clearly what it wanted. Under all changes of dynasty and circumstances the object of building up national power was kept in view; and Economics, though not yet admitted to the circle of the sciences, proved an excellent servant, and gave admirable suggestions as to the manner in which this aim might be accomplished. Since 1815 there has been a revulsion of feeling. It seemed to the ordinary Englishman unnecessary to go on building up additional securities of maritime power at a time when there were no rivals who seemed worth consideration. At the same time attention was consciously directed to another object, which had been neglected in the last days of the Mercantile System. Robert Owen gave an extraordinary impulse to the philanthropic movements of his time by setting himself to bring about the harmony of industrial progress and human welfare. The well-being of the masses of the people has become, in the eyes of many, the supreme object to which national activities should be directed; and in so far as this is a matter of material conditions —food, shelter, health, and leisure—Economic Science is an excellent help to shew us how far this object has been attained, and in what directions it may be most easily promoted.

In order to enquire into our success in attaining this result we naturally fix our attention on the evidence of the consumption of wealth, the amounts of the necessaries and conveniences of life which have been at the command of the community generally. This mode of examining the subject seems, in a democratic age, to be eminently fair. Consumption is a matter in which the whole community are directly interested. When we look at the production of wealth we obviously have to do with distinct interests, and possibly with conflicting interests. Not all the inhabitants of a country are engaged in the production of material wealth, and the welfare of some classes of producers, or some factors in the productive process, may be procured at the expense of other persons and classes. Ample opportunity for consumption, therefore, appears to afford the best test of the welfare of the community generally, and of every individual member severally. For the purpose of the examination of actual and observed phenomena this point of view serves admirably[1]. In modern times, and especially for the

---

[1] The method must of course be used with discrimination; the mere cheapness of commodities does not shew that they have been generally available for the labouring classes, unless the opportunities of employment and power of obtaining the means of purchasing

last half century, when masses of accurate data are available, enquiries as to the command possessed by the community in general, and the working classes in particular, over the conveniences and comforts of life can be pursued with considerable accuracy. We have means of measuring the material progress of the community in the recent past that are reliable so far as they go.

The question that the public desire to discuss, however, is not merely as to the manner in which things have worked in the past, but rather as to the prospects of their working well in the future ; how far is the welfare of the masses of the community likely to be maintained in the next and subsequent generation ? When we come to gauge the probabilities in the future the case is not easily settled. Account must be taken of the characteristic limitations of Economic Science, as compared with physical science; since the subject-matter is always changing[1] the accurate measurement of progress in the past does not give us a sound basis for estimating progress in the future. We need to get as close as we can to actuality in order to make a forecast of events with any high probability. The mechanical view of human life, which Economics assumes for purposes of clear analysis[2], is inappropriate when we are trying to look ahead ; the continued supply of the comforts and

food have also been considered. The insufficient attention paid by Professor Thorold Rogers to this point has greatly affected the value of his elaborate researches.

[1] See above, p. 129.   [2] See above, p. 5.

conveniences of life depends on the satisfactory interworking of production and exchange and consumption in society, not on any one stage in the economic process. The amount available for consumption cannot be taken as in itself a crucial test; it is only one symptom among others by which we can judge whether the economic life of the community is in a healthy condition or not. Farther than this, we may see that it is a particularly uninstructive symptom; consumption is a necessary element in the production of wealth, and in the enjoyment of life; but consumption is not in itself a good thing.

The production of utilities is likely to benefit somebody somehow; but consumption is not necessarily a benefit to anyone; it may possibly be another name for waste. The worst blunder of the Mercantilists in the seventeenth century arose in connection with this very point; they seemed to hold that by promoting consumption they were bringing about the increase of wealth. On this account the Parliament of England insisted that all Englishmen should be buried in wool, and the Parliament of Scotland that all Scotchmen should be buried in linen; another Black Death would have stimulated the demand for the staple manufactures of each country enormously; but increased rapidity of consumption is not a safe index to the growth of national wealth. Statistics of national consumption do not give us any information as to how the goods have been obtained, or as to whether they are being wisely used or foolishly wasted; and such information is essential, if we are to interpret the meaning of increased consumption as a symptom of the healthiness of our economic life.

In our present conditions, as a commercial and manufacturing people, the possibilities of continuing to procure food and materials for our consumption depends upon our trade ; a great part of the comforts and conveniences of life which we have been enjoying in such large measure comes from abroad ; and the statistics of our import trade are very well worth our consideration. At first sight they seem to afford ground for complete satisfaction : we are not only able to purchase great quantities of goods from abroad, in spite of all the hostile tariffs, but we are able to procure them on very easy terms. Besides the goods we export to discharge our debts for what we receive, there is an enormous mass of goods over and above which we do not seem to pay for in any tangible form. There is a large and increasing balance of imports over and above our exports. It would be a mistake to suppose that these goods are presented to England by rival traders, eagerly competing for the favour of her custom—as enterprising American shopkeepers will offer you a copy of *Robert Elsmere* if you are kind enough to purchase two pounds of their English breakfast tea. The excess of imports is payment, not for goods received by foreign countries but for services rendered to them. A large amount of capital has been invested in developing the resources of other lands, and this enables us to obtain considerable payments of interest every year. Besides this we own a very large proportion of the carrying trade of the world. A great deal of international commerce is carried on in English ships; and the payments for freight and insurance go to swell the mass of imports which reach us annually. There is to many people a satisfaction in being able to say that we are earning the large annual income we receive in the form of imports from foreign countries with comparatively little manual drudgery of our own; but I am not sure that it is a cause for self-gratulation. We can hardly be satisfied to be the remittance-man of the world, while others are pressing on through their activity and enterprise. It is obvious that the continuance of this large mass of imports, and the stability of the material welfare of our population, depends partly on the willingness of foreign countries to continue to pay us for our goods and for our services, and also, on the vigour of English economic life and the maintenance of our ability to meet their requirements. We cannot afford to let these faculties become dormant or fall out of use.

While a large importation from abroad is essential to our very existence as a community it seems improbable that foreign countries and our own colonies, with their great and undeveloped resources, will continue to rely indefinitely on English goods, and on the use of English capital and English shipping. If anyone should insist that other countries were developing so fast that our facilities for purchasing food and materials would be sensibly curtailed within the next five-and-twenty years—with consequent distress to the consumers of such imported commodities as corn—it would not be easy to prove that he was mistaken. In any case, this is a question of time, sooner or later; and it is hardly a manly course to be content to let things drift because there will not be much change for the worse 'in our days.' Hezekiah's thanksgiving—in all its unctuousness and all its meanness—that he would himself be spared any actual experience of the misery which was coming on his city, finds an echo in Little Englander utterances to-day. If we have any genuine patriotism we shall wish to face the situation, and to make up our minds as to whether the danger is so imminent that we would be wise to take account of it, and guard against it, if we can.

It is obvious that foreign nations are no longer dependent upon us for manufactured goods in anything like the degree in which they were fifty years ago. It was possible to anticipate at that time that a great system of international co-operation would be developed; that England would undertake any manufacturing that was required by the world at large, and that other peoples would prefer to spend their days in homely and rural occupations. They have abjured the scheme of international co-operation, and entered the field of industrial competition. They are proving themselves successful competitors; the pre-eminence which England enjoyed in the production of pig-iron has been secured by the United States, and England is being beaten by Germany[1] in the contest for the

[1] *Report on the Tariff Commission*, I. 33.

second place. The old-established staple trades
of the country are being cut into very seriously
indeed.

When we look more closely, we may notice that
the commodity which other nations are most eager to
procure from us is one which in the nature of things
we cannot continue indefinitely to supply. Coal is
the item in our exports which is steadily increasing
every year; it is becoming an important element in
our power of purchasing the supplies we need[1]. It
is clear, however, that not only is this mineral, like
other minerals, exhausted by the process of being
worked, but the beds of the steam-coal, which is so
much in demand, are comparatively small, and our
power of meeting this particular form of foreign
demand is correspondingly limited.

The growth of competition in the shipping trades
is also a serious prospect; there has been a sufficient
change of maritime routes to divert much of the trade
which formerly centred at the port of London; intercourse between Germany and the East is no longer

[1] "During 1883–92 as compared with 1873–82 our coal exports increased by £40,000,000, and our exports other than
coal increased ¦by £101,000,000. But during 1893–1902 as compared with 1883–92 our exports of coal increased by £84,000,000,
and our exports other than coal increased by only £28,000,000. I
may say here that even this small increase of £28,000,000 in our
exports other than coal was caused by the increase in our exports
of machinery and mill-work during 1893–1902, an increase of
£36,000,000. So that without this increase in our exports of
machinery our exports other than coal and machinery actually de-
creased by £8,000,000 during 1893–1902 as compared with
1883—1892." J. H. Schooling in *Journal of Royal Statistical
Society*, LXVII. 82.

carried on by the Channel and the Cape, but by
Italian ports and the Suez Canal[1], and there is an
increasing amount of direct traffic between America
and the Mediterranean. The rate of the growth of
foreign shipping does not reveal the full extent of the
danger ; a great commercial power is specially liable
to suffer irreparably in disturbed political conditions.
During the long wars English shipping suffered
severely, and high insurance rates were charged
because of the risks that had to be run ; the neutral
traders were at an enormous advantage. The case
might easily recur ; if England were involved in a
war, even for a brief period, with some maritime power,
the ships of any neutral state would have an enormous
advantage in securing increased trade ; and there
might be very serious difficulty in attracting commerce
back to the old channels when peace was restored[2].
So far as our imports depend on the service rendered
by this country to foreign traders, there is no great

[1] Nasse, *Ein Blick auf die kommerzielle und industrielle
Lage Englands* in Conrad's *Jahrbücher für Nationalökonomie und
Statistic.* N. F. xiv. 100.

[2] Since the above was written an excellent illustration has
been furnished by the following sentences from the *Times*, 11 Aug.,
1904. " The virtual withdrawal from the Japan service by the P.
& O., Holt, Thompson, and other leading English Companies leaves
the bulk of the carrying trade to the far East in the hands of two
or three firms of lesser importance. Even these latter are sorely
perplexed as to the choice of cargo, and large consignments of rails,
wire netting, and similar goods have been refused within the last
few days...German shipping-houses in Antwerp allow themselves
more latitude with regard to their freight list, while vessels
privately chartered, which have little to lose, are also stepping into
the breach to the detriment of the British carrying trade."

improbability that they may be able before long to dispense with it.

Nor is it quite certain that the income from English savings already invested in foreign countries will continue to be as large as it is at present. Many men who have retired from business find that from one cause or another the return on their savings shrinks, and that they undergo losses which they have no means of making up. Securities which carried a high rate of interest are paid off, and the money can only be re-invested at a reduced rate ; that is a frequent experience among individuals ; and it may easily have its analogue in national history. There is such a wide diffusion of commercial facilities and commercial habits that there are opportunities for forming capital in all parts of the world ; and as the less highly developed countries form their own stock, they will be in a position to pay lower interest to foreign borrowers, and eventually to pay them off altogether. The possession of large funds invested abroad is not a guarantee of continued income ; it is necessary that additional capital should be formed, and should find remunerative investment if this source of income is to be maintained unimpaired.

Even though it be true that additional capital is being formed and sent abroad, it is clear that the process cannot be going on very rapidly ; capital goes abroad in the form of exports, and large investment of capital abroad would reduce the excess of imports over exports. On the other hand there have been years when the excess of imports has suddenly increased; and this indicates that wealth is being brought home in masses and suggests that at the time we were forced to live upon our capital. In the year 1877, according to well-informed opinion in Liverpool, we saved ourselves from a great financial crisis by a large sacrifice of capital, especially of capital locked up in foreign securities and released at a considerable loss[1]. Two years later similar difficulties occurred; there was a terribly bad harvest in this country, and we imported corn in large quantities from the States, while at the same time large remittances of gold were made to that country[2]. When the excess of imports is suddenly increased owing to a loss of wealth in this country, and the deficiency is made up by realising securities in other countries, it is difficult to shew that we are not at that time and for that year trenching on our capital, instead of adding to it[3].

The evidence which goes to shew that fresh capital is being rapidly formed in England at the present moment is not unimpeachable. This country is becoming more and more the playground of the world. Men who have made their money in the colonies or in America pay long visits here and settle; the transference of a few millionaires from New York to London may cause a vast difference in the income remitted to this country; even though

[1] *Liverpool Daily Post*, 10 Jan. 1877.

[2] *Journal of the Statistical Society*, XLIII. 105, 107. Similar conditions recurred in 1880. Peez, *Zur neuesten Handelspolitik*, 87. The year 1891 was another year of poor crops, which shewed a sudden increase of the excess of imports.

[3] Fuchs, *Die Handelspolitik Englands*, p. 172.

the capital has all been formed, and the employment
it gives is all opened up, on the other side of the
world.

For after all it is on the active elements in
economic life—labour and enterprise—that continued
prosperity depends. Statistics of consumption tell
us little or nothing, unless we can supplement them
by information as to the opportunities and terms of
employment: how far is the wealth which comes here
to be consumed used for the production of more
wealth? It must be admitted that there is little sign
of enlarged fields for the employment of English
labour being opened up; the demand abroad for
English staple commodities is not increasing. Trade
is not reacting on home-industry, as it did in the
Fifties and Sixties to give it a stimulus. Under
the circumstances it cannot be said that the welfare
of our large population is at all secure.

(b) The economic expert, who desires to serve
the State, need not confine himself to discharging the
ungrateful task of a critic. There is ample room for
his assistance in connection with every department of
national activity. Economic study in its modern
form does not exclude any tribe or community from
its scope; and as it thus strives to co-ordinate such
varied information, it can give us valuable suggestions
as to almost any situation in actual life[1]. There is
nothing new under the sun; the requirements of
human beings are common to all ages, and the modes

---

[1] Cunningham, *Plea for the Study of Economic History* in
Economic Review, IX. 70.

of supplying wants which served in the past may sometimes be adapted to meet new conditions. Man is a rational animal, and experience acquired in other times or ages may be applied, with more or less modification, in the larger communities which enjoy in the twentieth century such largely extended powers over nature. The economic expert may be rightly appealed to for practical suggestions, as to the means by which any community may utilise its resources, so as to obtain the most of the thing it wants.

The object in view may be political or social— military power, scientific progress, diffused education. In each case the assistance of the expert may be called in, to estimate the expense which must be incurred for the end in view. If military power—on the scale on which it is desired—involves compulsory military service on the part of all citizens, the expense of diverting them from industrial pursuits during the periods of military training, as well as the actual cost of the maintenance of the army, must be estimated. On the other hand, the indirect benefits to economic life, which are sometimes said to arise from military training and discipline, as well as the public security which the army may ensure, though more remote results, must not be overlooked. In such cases it is the function of the expert to shew how the burden of increased military organisation may be most conveniently borne.

Again, the object in view may be economic— the development of the resources of the country and the stimulating the vigour and enterprise of its inhabitants. It is possible that if there were a perfectly free flow of labour and capital to all parts of the world there might never be either the occasion or opportunity to take active measures to foster industry and commerce. But in the world as we know it that is not the case; some countries are sparsely inhabited and do not attract many settlers, or they are peopled by races who have little aptitude for the forms of enterprise for which the area is physically well adapted. There is much that can be done by active measures to hasten the slow process by which labour and capital find their way to new regions, and thus to start industries much more early than would otherwise be possible. Even though a considerable outlay may be necessary, success in establishing one branch of a really suitable industry will probably react favourably on the whole economic condition of the community.

Another problem on which the advice of the economic expert may be sought with advantage is that of minimising the social evils of some necessary transition. In modern times there is very little stability about any business; the progress of invention and discovery is making constant differences in the arts; trade has its ups and downs, and there are changes in the localisation of industry which leave many persons stranded. The misery which accrued from the substitution of machine spinning of wool for hand work was doubtless alleviated by the expedient of granting allowances from wages; but it is to be noticed that one method of interference is likely to be more prejudicial than others. Had it been possible to organise fresh forms of employment, rather than to provide money doles, the benefit would have been equally great, but more indirect and less pauperising. In the same way it appears that the effort to stimulate industry by keeping prices high and the rate of profits good—as may be done by tariffs—is less wholesome than the indirect stimulus which arises from opening up new markets and thus increasing the demand. The modern economic expert is likely to follow the example of modern medical practice, and to rely less on occasional doses of powerful drugs than on the restorative powers of nature. The system of Natural Liberty is the one which Adam Smith recommended as most likely to cure occasional mischief without any possible injury to the constitution.

iii. *State Regulation.*

It is of course perfectly true that ill-judged interference by the State with industry and trade is mischievous[1]. Men like Mr Bumble, who think that "the law is a hass" and that all legislatures are corrupt, are inclined to maintain the thesis that any interference is necessarily wrong. But after all, there is no choice in the matter ; the different sides of life are so closely interconnected that political and social

---

[1] The encouragement given by the mother country to the Canadians to develop the lumber trade, and exploit natural productions rather than develop tillage, was a case in point. Shortt, *Imperial Preferential Trade*, 25.

requirements necessitate some interference, much or
little; the question is as to its quality, good or bad.
It is idle to suppose that we have succeeded in
realising a condition in which the State does not interfere with the course of trade. There are numerous
subsidies to shipping firms, partly for public convenience and the maintenance of a rapid mail
service, and partly with a view to military exigencies.
The duties on foreign spirits and beer appear to be
inconsistent with thoroughgoing Free Trade[1]; the
interests of sobriety, and the desirability of levying
countervailing duties so as to give fair play to
producers at home, have been taken into account as
well as considerations of revenue. Special restrictions
on the manner in which the retailing of alcoholic
liquors is carried on have given rise to special
legislation in the interest of the holders of public-
house property. By making the principle of non-
interference, in an exaggerated form, the forefront
of our economic scheme, we have given an excuse
for riddling it with exceptions. The whole thing is
a sham; each threatened interest endeavours to make
out a case for enjoying exceptional treatment; and
protection is being gradually introduced in its worst,
because its least considered forms. The best remedy
for the mischief which accrues from haphazard interference with trade is to be found in taking constant
and habitual care of it on well-considered principles[2].

[1] Fuchs, *Die Handelspolitik Englands*, 17, 47.

[2] Compare Adam Smith's contrast between the legislator who
is guided by principles and the insidious animal who follows the
momentary fluctuations of affairs. Cunningham, *Richard Cobden
and Adam Smith*, 24.

The fear that if attention were habitually given
to the regulation of trade there would be a seriously
increased danger of corruption appears to be illusory ;
it rests, like the doctrine of the deadening effects of
protection on enterprise, on a mere theory of human
nature, and not on observed fact.   There is no
necessary connection between State-management of
trade and corruption ; under the Long Parliament
and Council of State, when *laissez-faire* principles
were generally adopted, corruption of every kind was
rampant.   Cromwell shewed his strength in getting
rid of the worst offenders, and he reversed their policy
and re-established the East India Company on a joint-
stock basis, and other exclusive companies to carry
on a well-ordered trade.   A more modern illustration
is offered by the United States ; the triumph of the
Free Trade party is the recognised era of the begin-
nings of the systematic lowering of the standard of
political life : the cry of " The spoils to the Victors "
was raised in 1831 after the election of Jackson to
the Presidency. Carelessness is not necessarily favourable either to prosperity or to virtue.

There is indeed a wide-spread superstition that if
things are only left alone they are sure to work out
in the best possible way and to the greatest happiness
of the greatest number. Reliance on unrestricted
individual competition—the war of all with all—
as the essential condition of improvement appears to
derive some support from the Darwinian doctrine of
the survival of the fittest.   But physical nature
and human society are so far distinct spheres that

we cannot argue directly from one to the other.
Individual competition is only a beneficent force
when the conditions under which it acts are carefully
controlled; the legal system of the country exists for
the very purpose of putting down methods of individual competition, which can be branded as dishonest
and injurious to the public. The malign effects, so
far as the welfare of any one community is concerned,
of reckless competition may be seen in the waste of
natural resources, both as regards forests and fisheries, in the degradation of the labourers' standard
of life during the first quarter of the nineteenth
century, and at times in the deterioration of the
quality of wares. All these phenomena are likely
to recur when "things are in the saddle and ride
mankind."

After all, man has enough intelligence to be capable
of accumulating a body of knowledge as to the best
way of utilising physical resources to his permanent
advantages; collective wisdom is not unattainable.
It is possible to organise human activity so that the
best results shall be obtained from the soil without
exhausting it; it is possible to take active measures
for improving the population, both physically and
mentally. Steady and persistent effort may accomplish much even in the oldest country, and among
races suffering from centuries of oppression. The
work of England for the regeneration of Egypt may
serve to remind us how much may be accomplished, not by letting things drift, but by taking
pains.

CHAPTER VII.

AN IMPERIAL SYSTEM.

i. *Looking backward.*

IT is obvious enough that there are serious grounds
for dissatisfaction with our present scheme of one-
sided Free Trade. It is artificial; it tends to foster
a redundant population; it has not created mutual
interdependence among nations, but has instead
rendered England economically dependent on foreign
countries which are no longer within the sphere of her
industrial influence. Still, it may be asked, are these
faults in our present scheme, however grave they may
be, reasons for going back to a bad system which we
had discarded? Certainly not. Nobody wishes to go
back to the old scheme; we aim at constructing a
new system with the help of experience we have
acquired not only under the Mercantile *régime*, but
under that of one-sided Free Trade.

The proposal to work for the better organisation
of the economic life of the British Empire as a whole
assumes a very different political basis from that of
the Mercantile System which was finally swept away in

the Forties. The old system was built up on a national basis—England or Great Britain; it deliberately subordinated the interests of Englishmen in other regions to those of the mother country, and especially to the maintenance of the revenue of the mother country; under Free Trade, our economic policy has continued to be insular; the United Kingdom is a "small State." The Imperial system will regard the mother country as only a part, though at present the most prominent part, of a Greater Britain, and will endeavour to see that every portion of the Empire shall be enabled to use its opportunities of rapid progress along the lines which are marked out for it by its physical resources and situation. We shall thus have a natural, not an artificial system. This conception of the solidarity of interests between the various members of one body, on which the new proposal depends, is entirely inconsistent with that balancing of British and colonial interests which was the cause of so much mutual jealousy and irritation in the past. We may frankly recognise the principle which Huskisson laid down, "that whatever tends to increase the prosperity of the colonies cannot fail in the long run to advance in an equal degree the general interests of the parent state[1]." We hope to create a strong and prosperous Empire, but we cannot take a single step in this direction till we shake off the trammels of insular Free Trade. We cannot hope to evoke much response from the colonies, until we shew that we are prepared to act in our own interests; we

[1] *Speeches*, II. 314.

must assume such a position that we shall be free to
bargain with foreign Powers by treaty, and if necessary
to retaliate upon them, before the colonies can feel
that their interests are safe in our hands. We
must be free to grant preferences to the colonies
on supplies of food and raw produce. If we take
this bold line, we run some risk of temporary loss;
but we may hope to re-establish English influence
in the world, on a more natural, and therefore a
firmer basis than ever. The *famille souche*, which
has given the guarantee of continued well-being in
many communities[1], is a type which may be repro-
duced in modern world politics. The multiplicity
and variety of our colonies and dependencies are not a
source of weakness. "Blessed is the nation that hath
her quiver full of them. She shall not be ashamed
to speak with her enemies in the gate."

The principle on which the old methods of regulation depended was that of authority ; a new organisation can only be built up by the co-operation of
free peoples. From this point of view we may see
that Pitt's proposal for granting greater economic
freedom to the colonies was premature : it might
have been a positive hindrance to their political development. Even Huskisson's statesmanlike scheme
of preferences gave occasion for disastrous meddling
with the internal affairs of the plantations by the
Colonial Office[2] ; it was only when his scheme was

[1] "Stable à son Foyer, alliant la Tradition et la Nouveauté."
Le Play, *Les Ouvriers Européens*, I. 457.
[2] Davidson, *Commercial Federation*, 6, 19.

brushed away by Peel, and the colonies were cut adrift economically so that we might pursue the Free Trade policy unhindered, that the need for granting them responsible government came to be seriously considered. However much we may now regret that Huskisson's system of preference was not developed rather than destroyed, we can see that the clean sweep which was made of the colonial and navigation system leaves the field free, not for mere adaptation, but for reconstruction on lines that are obviously new. Co-operation between the mother country and the colonies may be of vast advantage, for each has much to give to the other. England has had long practice in the art of self-government, and fosters a high sense of public duty; the colonies have infinite possibilities of development in the future; it were idle to weigh one element against the other, or say which is more essential to the continued prosperity of the Empire, but each part can contribute much to the common weal.

Those who are really in earnest about this matter will not be satisfied with mere talk about Imperial sentiment and Colonial loyalty. Sentimental attachments may be very warm, but they are not to be depended on by themselves: a comparatively small cause of irritation will lead to a rupture. The mere sentiment will become more reliable if it is strengthened by ties of mutual interest[1]. Cobden

---

[1] "The greater reliability of ties of interest is brought out in the history of the unification of Germany. The growth of the Empire out of the Zollverein has proved that a cash nexus is the safest

was right in thinking that he could transfuse the forms of democratic government in England with real life by arousing the citizens to a sense of their interests. Imperial sentiment is to be highly prized, but it will not enable us to dispense with organisation; a beginning has been made with efforts at Imperial co-operation for purposes of defence; and Imperial co-operation for economic purposes is hardly of secondary importance. In both cases an advisory council, in which all the colonies should be able to make their voice heard, would be able to recommend lines of action which the various responsible Governments might wisely carry into effect. On whatever lines the political life of the Empire shall be fashioned, the economic life must be similarly organised, so that the two sides may be adapted to each other. When we realise how much the various parts of the Empire can do for one another, the desire to secure co-operation for mutual advantage as a permanent thing will find expression naturally in attempts at Imperial economic organisation.

Eighty years ago Mr E. G. Wakefield pointed out how well suited England and the colonies were to supplement one another. England had a large popu-

road to political unity. Austria, the natural and historic leader of German-speaking peoples, despised all such sordid bonds, and trusted to sentiment, to diplomacy, and to the remembrance of past headship. Prussia, with far-seeing patience, and at the cost of many pecuniary sacrifices and the frequent subordination of her immediate interests, built up the system which joined the scattered and hostile German States through a customs union into that Empire which had seemed the most impossible of dreams." J. Parker Smith in *Broad Views*, May, 1904.

lation, and great accumulations of capital ; while the colonies had vast expanses of land : the three main factors in production were amply available in one or the other[1]. We have yet to learn how to make the most of these resources. In the years that have elapsed since his time there has been a constant stream of immigration from our shores ; numbers of excellent labourers and artisans have gone abroad, but there has been no sufficient attention to the desirability of retaining them under the English flag, and utilising their energies to develop the resources of the Empire. In a similar way, English capital has been invested in all parts of the world ; it has been used to open up communications and plant manufactures in foreign countries, and thus to build up the military and industrial power of our rivals, when it might have been employed more advantageously to the common weal, in developing parts of our own Empire. England has been lacking in ordinary prudence in thus neglecting to do what lay to hand for the economic prosperity of the colonies ; but it is not too late to take a new line for the future. The distribution of the population of the Empire, to those areas where it can be most suitably employed, may be systematically undertaken. The colonies are rightly unwilling to be a dumping ground for the dregs of European cities[2] ; but it may not be impossible to

---

[1] Wakefield, *Art of Colonisation*, 91.

[2] " In the younger colonies of the Empire population is essential, and if increased from British stock the self-governing colonies will still further strengthen and buttress our great Empire. In British in-

divert the stream of desirable adult emigrants to our own colonies, or to provide for the nurturing and transshipment of children, who may grow up under more healthy surroundings than they enjoy in our towns.

The colonies are as yet insufficiently supplied with capital; they are endeavouring to attract it to the development of their industries by protective tariffs, which are intended to secure a higher rate of profit for the investor. Particular English traders may find themselves injured by colonial tariffs, but the policy, which the colonists are adopting, opens up a field for English investors who desire a higher rate of interest than they can obtain from secured investments in municipal bonds. Colonial protection is not detrimental to English capital which is seeking remunerative employment anywhere under the English flag. Frank recognition of the independence of the colonies is not inconsistent with the encouragement of conscious co-operation. In so far as the colonies and the mother country can work together for mutual advantage, ties of interest will grow up to strengthen, but not to take the place of common sentiment. The same principle of mutual helpfulness which Cobden recommended to the world as a whole, may be usefully applied, so far as circumstances allow, within the area of the British Empire.

terests it is clearly undesirable that the colonies should become populated by the inferior surplus of peoples of older and alien countries. To prevent such a disaster is worthy of our best thoughts and most strenuous efforts." Mr Seddon in the *Daily Express*, 22 Aug. 1904.

ii. *Cosmopolitan Competition.*

In attempting to devise a new scheme of economic policy much may be learned from Cobden's failure to bring about universal free intercourse. The reason of his disappointment is not far to seek; we must endeavour to keep clear of the barrier which first checked and then repelled the advancing Free Trade movement. Implicitly and from the first the doctrine had been cosmopolitan; it "took no account of nations, but simply of the entire human race on one hand, or of single individuals on the other[1]." In so far as it was brought into practice in the nineteenth century foreign countries were placed on the defensive; they felt that they were being crowded out of their due place in the world by British aggression. That this aggression took place at the instance of a peace-at-any-price party, who were accustomed to declaim against extensions of English military power and prestige, did not render it less offensive. The Manchester men, with all their professions of peace, were the cause of irritating other nations into retaliation. Foreign statesmen saw that English capital and enterprise would flow past them to develop distant lands and establish British influence on a secure foundation throughout the whole globe. "Asia, Africa, and Australia would be civilized by England, and covered with new states modelled after the English fashion.

---

[1] List, *National System of Political Economy*, p. xxvi.; and Fuchs, *op. cit.*, p. 4.

In time a world of English states would be formed under the presidency of the mother state, in which the European continental nations would be lost as unimportant, unproductive races. By this arrangement it would fall to the lot of France, together with Spain and Portugal, to supply this English world with the choicest wines, and to drink the bad ones herself; at most France might retain the manufacture of a little millinery. Germany would scarcely have more to supply this English world with than children's toys, wooden clocks and philological writings, and sometimes also an auxiliary corps who might sacrifice themselves to pine away in the deserts of Asia or Africa, for the sake of extending the manufacturing and commercial supremacy, the literature and language of England. It would not require many centuries before people in this English world would think and speak of the Germans and French in the same tone as we speak at present of the Asiatic nations. True political science, however, regards such a result of universal Free Trade as a very unnatural one; it will argue that had universal Free Trade been introduced at the time of the Hanseatic League, the German nationality instead of the English would have secured an advance in commerce and manufacture over all other countries[1]." There need be no wonder that Cobden and his contemporaries were glad to dispense with the colonies, since care for them was an obstacle to the scheme which offered good prospects of anglicising the whole globe.

[1] List, *op. cit.*, 130.

Cobden is not the only professed peace-maker who has found that the measures by which he intended to allay jealousy have aggravated and intensified the difference. He had hoped that, as a result of free intercourse, all the countries of the world would agree to co-operate for the common good ; but he did not introduce national co-operation; he only widened the range of individual competition, until it became a danger to national life. The Zollverein and the protective system in the United States were definitely intended to check the deadening influence which English industry and commerce were exercising upon our neighbours. The tariffs were devised in accordance with the principles of List, who held that "in order to allow freedom of trade to operate naturally, the less advanced nations must first be raised by artificial measures to that stage of cultivation to which the English nation has been artificially elevated[1]." He believed in reciprocal Free Trade ; that is in intercourse between such communities as would each gain in their social and economic life from such free communication. He did not approve of Free Trade in the sense of allowing an economically strong country to crush others that were, at the time, economically weak. It would perhaps be unjust to say that this was what Cobden and his followers desired to do, but certainly other countries felt that this was what English Free Trade tended to do. In the light of that experience we cannot even desire that there should be such a rigid system of Free Trade within the Empire, as

[1] List, *op. cit.*, 131.

would bring a deadening influence to bear on the advance of the colonies.

The malign effects of cosmopolitan competition are beginning to shew themselves in another way; since we find that racial struggles are breaking out more bitterly in the industrial world. The standard of comfort of the white man and the black is not the same ; unfettered competition between individuals of different races tends to the degradation of the standard of comfort which is characteristic of the higher civilisation. It is on this account that the Australian colonies and the United States are so eager to protect themselves against the immigration of the yellow races ; and the outbreak of anti-Semitic crusades in other countries can be traced in part to a similar feeling. So far as our staple industries are concerned, the danger of race-competition cannot be met by checking the incursion of undesirables. During the last fifty years the status and standard of comfort of the English labourers have improved immensely ; it almost seems as if we had been engaged in the 'scientific protection' of the working man. He has better clothes, food and shelter, and immensely increased leisure ; he does not always use this last as well as he might, but he has at least the opportunity of mental improvement which leisure affords. We are still busy devising technical schools that shall train men to work; we have not yet had time to tackle the more difficult educational problem of teaching the masses to use their leisure to the best advantage[1].

[1] Cunningham, *Gospel of Work*, 130.

The combined efforts of their own associations and of factory legislation have raised the standard of comfort of the Lancashire factory operatives to a very high plane. But it is doubtful if this can be maintained in the face of cosmopolitan competition. Lancashire has not merely to hold her own against the skill in organisation and the intense application of Germans, and of operatives in Massachusetts, but against the factories in South Carolina[1], where 'mean whites' are employed. The conditions of work to which the hands are forced to submit seem to be as bad as anything that occurred in the unregulated mills of the early nineteenth century[2]; and the standard of comfort of people who are habituated to a warm climate is much lower than that which obtains in Lancashire. There is a danger that the position of the labourer in civilised countries will be seriously injured, if the Englishman is not careful to protect himself against the malign results of cosmopolitan competition.

The sense of the danger which lurks in cosmopolitan competition may help to give us a new sense of Imperial duty. While the white man is prudent to protect himself, he is equally bound to see that the less vigorous and aggressive races do not suffer through the new conditions which follow as the circle of commerce expands. As new countries are opened up, and drawn within the sphere of international commerce, they offer a field for the organisation of

[1] Helm, *Survey of Cotton Industry* in *Quarterly Journal of Economics*, xvii. 428.

[2] B. and M. van Vorst, *The Woman Who Toils*, 281.

industry on modern methods by capitalists. It may be rural labour on plantations, or extractive labour in mines, or industrial in factories ; but when we remember that there was need for the regulation of the conditions of white labour under capitalist employers in English factories and mines, we may see that there is even greater danger of the oppression of coloured labour by European capitalists in tropical lands. It is the privilege of the white man to protect himself, and it is his duty to see that native races and imported coolies are not exploited by their employers[1]. The labour problems in the different parts of the Empire can never be satisfactorily solved unless measures can be taken to check the competition of the black man with the white ; and this involves the assignment of certain occupations to each, if both are to live side by side in the same territory. It has been the mark of English rule in all parts of the world that the Government has endeavoured to preserve the culture and traditions of native races, and to give them the opportunity of making the most of themselves. Cosmopolitan competition allows each country to exert a deleterious influence on its neighbours ; the strong to depress the weak, and the poor to drag down others to their own level. It is the task of Imperial administration to endeavour to give fair play to all these various elements, so that the best qualities of each race may be brought into play.

[1] Alleyne Ireland, *Tropical Civilisation*, 164.

iii. *The result of the survey.*

The course which has been run by the Free
Trade movement, during the nineteenth century, is
clearly marked. We have traced the progress which
it made, not only in England, but in commercial
countries generally until about 1870, and the decline
which has taken place since that decade.   The
doctrine, which was set forth with so much confidence,
has been tested by the logic of events; it has been
discarded by the countries that are growing most
rapidly in wealth and power. Yet for all that the
principles of Free Trade remain unshaken; we may
still keep to the opinion that Free Trade is economically advantageous to the world as a whole, and to
consumers individually at any given moment.   The
benefits it offers are much to be desired, but only in
so far as they are compatible with the development
of civilised life in all parts of the globe, and do not
tend to the depression or disintegration of independent political communities.   The real, though
incidental, disadvantages which accrued through the
advance of Free Trade are well worth taking into
account; for they help us to understand the circumstances in which Free Trade principles can be
beneficially applied.   Cobden was an enthusiast for
unconditional Free Trade; he thought that if free
intercourse were adopted it would make suitable social
and political conditions for itself and bring about
Universal Peace.   But he mistook cause for effect[1],

---

[1] List, *op. cit.*, 126.

or rather he failed to realise that the result he looked for could be best obtained, not by the stroke of a pen, but by the gradual interaction of economic forces and of political and social factors which he was inclined to disparage.

Under changed circumstances the old issues have disappeared, and the lines of cleavage which were drawn in 1846 no longer exist. Protectionists of the old type, who wished to retain in its main features the system under which English maritime supremacy was built up, have passed away, with the abolition of the scheme they prized so highly. We may all claim to be Free Traders in principle. The name has ceased to be really distinctive; the issues that lie before us are questions as to the conditions under which these principles may be wisely put into practice.

At a time when Scotland is so intent on events that occurred in the Forties, and is debating the question, Which is the genuine Free Church? we may perhaps put our enquiry in a similar form and ask, Who are the genuine Free Traders? But it is not easy to give a precise definition of orthodoxy; for, when we consider the matter, we see that there always have been, and are, two sorts of Free Traders —the *doctrinaire* and the *opportunist*.

The *doctrinaires* have not been very numerous in the sphere of practical politics; they are sufficiently represented by the author of the London Merchants' Petition[1], and Sir Robert Peel[2]. They are familiar figures among the bystanders who criticise public

[1] See above, p. 39.   [2] See above, p. 51.

affairs; they seem to regard Economic Science as a master[1] which lays down rules that should be followed to their logical issues; they appear to be content to live in a world of thought, clear and convincing, but illusory. In this attachment to their principles, they are prepared to abandon all the incidental advantages which Cobden prized so highly. They cannot deny that the world has turned against them; that England has ceased to be a leader which other nations are ready to copy; and that international antagonisms, and racial jealousies, have been the offspring of cosmopolitan competition. They see that there is no immediate hope of enlarging the circle of exchange, or increasing employment, by any step we can take; and that the economic benefits at which Cobden aimed cannot be increasingly obtained by his method. They profess to be content with the fact that for the present we are able to procure cheap food, and to manufacture at low prices—an ideal of economic welfare which Cobden explicitly repudiated[2].

But side by side with these *doctrinaires*, there has also been a long succession of eminent Free Traders who were *opportunists*, since they accepted Free Trade as a principle to be adopted as far as they found it to be expedient under the circumstances; but they claimed the right to judge of the circumstances for themselves. Huskisson was an opportunist; he was "not anxious to give effect to new principles when circumstances do not call for their application"; he felt "how much in the vast and

[1] See above, p. 126.   [2] See above, p. 60.

complicated interests of this country all general
theories, however incontrovertible in the abstract,
require to be weighed with a calm circumspection, to
be directed by a temperate discretion, and to be
adapted to all the existing relations of society with
a careful hand, and a due regard to the establishments
and institutions which have grown up under those
relations[1]." Cobden parted company with the *doctrinaires* when he negotiated the Treaty with France;
he did not take his stand upon the principle of free
intercourse when he saw that he could increase the
area within which it was practised. Gladstone was
another opportunist; yet these men are surely to be
reckoned as genuine Free Traders. Whatever we may
choose to call ourselves, or submit to be called at the
present time, we shall be well advised to follow the
method pursued by these leaders, and set ourselves
to think out carefully what course promises best
under existing circumstances.

Free Trade is not an absolute ideal, to be pursued
by all people under all conditions. It is not even a
sign of goodwill which the people of advanced communities can hold out to the inhabitants of less
developed countries; since it involves a "war of
all against all." Representative institutions are
an excellent thing, but they cannot be safely introduced in any State, without regard to the social
environment; and the case of Free Trade is similar.
There are large areas in Germany, Russia, and
America, each under the same political control, in

[1] *Speeches*, II. 305.

which free intercourse obtains. We should desist
from the attempt to apply the doctrine directly to
all parts of our Empire, and be content if we can so
increase the volume and range of commerce between
the countries under the British flag, that each may
prosper in itself and play an increasingly important
part in the life of the whole. The economic organisation of the Empire is needed, not only to introduce
a greater measure of free intercourse within its
bounds, but to be a bulwark against the evils of
cosmopolitan competition. A great Empire, thus
built up, need not exercise either a political or an
industrial tyranny over its neighbours, but may help
to serve as a foundation on which the Peace of the
World can rest securely. At all events, by introducing some economic order into the Empire we may
hope to secure a steadily increasing circle of exchange,
and to find a practical answer to a new form of
Cobden's question, In the face of cosmopolitan competition, how can English "wages be kept up, unless
there be constantly increasing markets found for the
employment of labour[1]"?

[1] Morley, *Life of Cobden*, I. 141.

THE REAL RICHARD COBDEN.

OF all the men who took a prominent part in English political life during the nineteenth century none appeals to the imagination of a subsequent age more strongly than Richard Cobden. He was of comparatively humble origin, with no special advantage of birth or education; and yet he was able to make a very deep mark on English history. Cobden must have been a man of remarkable force of character to achieve such success; his energy, his intellectual ability and strength of will were qualities which all Englishmen may fitly recognise and admire on the centenary of his birth. Unfortunately, however, his name has become so much of a party badge that there are many people who are only able to look at him through the spectacles of present-day politics. A legendary Cobden has been created. Those who claim to be his disciples appear to regard him as an embodiment of political wisdom, which holds good unaltered and unalterable from age to age; while Imperialists are too ready to denounce him as a charlatan who has proved himself a blind leader of the blind. Surely a hundred years after his birth, and thirty-nine after his death, it is possible to arrive at a more discriminating judgment, and to try to study the real man as he actually lived and worked. Men who are thoroughgoing in their Imperialism, and their advocacy of Tariff Reform, will find, if they examine the matter carefully, that they can sympathise much more completely with Richard Cobden in his aims and his principles than they might have been inclined to suppose.

I.

1. Imperialists in the present day can claim to be thoroughly democratic; the great campaign which Mr Chamberlain began in 1903 was an appeal to the masses of the people; and such an undertaking would hardly have been possible, but for the success of Cobden's efforts in awakening a widely diffused interest in public affairs. For Cobden was, before all else, intensely democratic; he had a horror of bureaucracy and all its ways. He entered public life at a time when the country was singularly apathetic; a great constitutional change had been accomplished by the Reform Bill of 1832, but those who had anticipated that this measure would be immediately followed by a sort of regeneration of national life were bitterly disappointed. Cobden believed in the sound common-sense of the enlarged electorate, and was at pains to incite them to exercise their privileges as citizens. He busied himself about the detail of political machinery, and especially insisted on the necessity of attending to registration; he was a

pioneer in the work of establishing effective organisation in large constituencies. In this connection he
realised that it would be worth while to engage in an
agitation against the Corn Laws. His interest in the
matter was primarily political, since he felt that this
topic might be so treated as to rouse Englishmen
generally to make use of their political rights. A
few sentences from one of his letters to his brother
may help to render his position clear. The present
Radical outbreak, he wrote in 1838, " is preferable to
the apathy of the three years when prosperity (or
seemingly so) made Tories of us all. Nor do I feel
at all inclined to give up politics in disgust, as you
seem to do because of the blunders of the Radicals.
They are rash and presumptuous, or ignorant if you
will, but are not the governing factions something
worse ? Is not selfishness, or systematic plunder, or
political knavery as odious as the blunders of
democracy ? We must choose between the party
which governs upon an exclusive or monopoly
principle, and the people who seek, though blindly
perhaps, the good of the vast majority. If they be
in error we must try to put them right, if rash to
moderate, but *never, never* talk of giving up the
ship. . . . *I think the scattered elements* may
yet be rallied round the question of the Corn Laws.
It appears to me that a moral and even a religious
spirit may be infused into that topic, and if agitated
in the same manner that the question of slavery has
been it will be irresistible[1]." Cobden's object was

[1] Morley's *Life of Cobden*, vol. I. p. 126.

one with which we can fully sympathise; he regarded this economic agitation as a means to a great political end. The question of the food supply was one in which he could interest his fellow-countrymen, and in regard to which they would respond. They would, as he hoped, arouse themselves to dispossess the oligarchy which had absorbed all legislative and administrative action, and to take the government of the country into their own hands.

The strength of Cobden's democratic enthusiasm accounts in some degree for the vehemence of the language he frequently used in regard to the Colonial system. The British Empire of to-day, embracing as it does so many self-governing communities, has lost the features which roused his indignation. Colonial government, as Cobden knew it, presented the least favourable aspect of the bureaucratic system he detested; and there seemed to be little hope that official routine could be so far modified that the Colonies would secure any real rights of self-government under the English crown. He was anxious that English settlers abroad should enjoy the full privileges of citizenship, and the continued authority of the Mother Country seemed to be an obstacle to the development of a true democracy. He apparently agreed with such economists as Dean Tucker and Sir John Sinclair in regarding the Colonies as a useless burden to the Mother Country, but his desire to cut them adrift was not merely selfish. He was eager to sever the tie with Great Britain for the sake of the Colonists themselves, in order that they might enjoy free institutions of their own. He was not wholly indifferent to the Colonies, for he wanted to see them democratic, and he recognised no advantage in maintaining a connection, which he regarded as an extravagance for the Mother Country and as mischievous to the Colonists. It is only as the system which repelled him has been replaced by responsible government in the Colonies themselves, that the Imperial sentiment, which we feel so strongly, has come into being.

2. There was another trait in Cobden's character, which is very noticeable all through his career. He was anxious to deal with actual affairs; he had no patience with mere phrases, and a profound contempt for party badges. To a genuine democrat, such as Cobden was, the Whig aristocrats, with their phrases about our glorious constitution, were particularly obnoxious, and he regarded them as his most dangerous enemies. The forms of government, to which they attached so much importance, were to his mind matters of little moment; in his enthusiasm over the efficiency of the Government in Prussia he was ready to pour scorn on the institutions they treated as sacred. "Had our people," he wrote[1], "such a simple and economical Government, so deeply imbued with justice to all, and aiming so constantly to elevate mentally and morally its population, how much better would it be for the twelve or fifteen millions in the British Empire, who, while they possess no electoral rights, are yet persuaded they are freemen, and who

[1] Morley's *Life of Cobden*, vol. I. p. 130.

are mystified into the notion that they are not
political bondmen, by that great juggle of the
English constitution—a thing of monopolies, and
Church-craft, and sinecures, armorial hocus-pocus,
primogeniture and pageantry." He was quite able
to appreciate good administration when he came
across it, whether that of a Prussian monarch or
a French Emperor, but he took no account of the
form of self-government without the power.

At a later period in his career Cobden was brought
into antagonism with the exponents of economic
theory. He was an opportunist, and when he saw
that a chance offered itself of extending commercial
intercourse with France, he grasped at it readily, and
set himself to carry through his commercial treaty,
even though it did not "sound in tune with the
verbal jingle of an abstract dogma[1]." He had been
willing to avail himself of the help of the economists
in the great agitation against the Corn Laws ; but the
doctrinaires, who were appealing to their favourite
formulæ to condemn a real advance in freedom of
intercourse, were treated with the contempt they
deserved[2]. With the attitude which Cobden assumed
in 1860 towards economic pedants and charlatans,
the Imperialists of the present day can cordially
sympathise. We are not going to be put off by mere
phrases in the controversy on which we have entered,
for we mean to insist on taking facts as they are, and
the world as we find it.

---

[1] Morley's *Life of Cobden*, vol. II. p. 343.
[2] *Ibid.* p. 338.

3. So far we have been considering Cobden's general habit of mind ; but there is one particular point to which it is worth while to direct special attention. He was quite decided in regarding the employment of labour and the employment of land as the true tests of national prosperity. The question as to the employment of labour was the gist of the whole matter in the attack he made on the Corn Laws. As Mr Morley summarises the situation, he was incessantly asking, "With a population increasing at the rate of a thousand souls a day, how can wages be kept up, unless there be constantly increasing markets found for the employment of labour ; and how can foreign countries buy our manufactures unless we take in return their corn, timber, or whatever else they are able to produce[1]?" He was aiming in the 'Forties at the very object which Tariff Reformers set before them now—the increase of employment by securing better markets. The means are different, but the end in view is the same.

Cobden's views on this topic are so entirely different from those of Twentieth Century "Free Fooders" that it is worth while to look at the matter somewhat closely. He distinctly repudiated the view, which is now put forward in his name, that the great thing is to make food cheap. He says : "We do not seek free trade in corn primarily for the purpose of purchasing it at a cheaper money rate[2]." He indignantly denied the allegation that the manu-

[1] Morley's *Life of Cobden*, vol. I. p. 141.
[2] July 3rd, 1844.—*Speeches*, vol. I. p. 208.

facturers were agitating for cheap food in the hope that their wages bill would be reduced. He held that the repeal of the Corn Laws would enable the manufacturers to "employ our people at good wages[1]." He blamed Sir Robert Peel for the mistake of resting the case for giving greater freedom to trade on any anticipated reduction of prices[2]. Cobden himself did not rest his case upon the cheapening of commodities to the consumer, but on the prospective increase of employment for the producer. "We believe that Free Trade will increase the demand for labour of every kind, not merely of the mechanical classes and those engaged in laborious bodily occupations, but for clerks, shopmen, and warehousemen, giving employment to all those youths whom you are so desirous of setting out in the world[3]." Further, he believed that this great development would come without any real injury to the agricultural interest. He held, on the one hand, that a large part of the population was so insufficiently fed, that an increase of employment and wages would lead to a greatly increased demand for corn; the half-starved labourers would then be able to buy as much as they wanted[4]. But while he looked forward to an increase in the effective demand, he did not foresee any likelihood of large supplies coming in at a greatly reduced price. The cost of transit from Dantzic was about 10*s*. 6*d*.

[1] *Speeches*, vol. I. p. 201.
[2] March 12th, 1844.—*Ibid.*, vol. I. p. 143. See above, p. 60.
[3] July 3rd, 1844.—*Ibid.*, vol. I. p. 205.
[4] January 15th, 1845.—*Ibid.*, vol. I. p. 253.

a quarter, and this was "the natural protection enjoyed by the farmers of this country[1]." And hence he honestly put forward a very roseate, and a very mistaken forecast of the probable future of English agriculture. "We are convinced," he says, that Free Trade in corn "will benefit the tenant farmer as much as any trader or manufacturer in the community. Neither do we believe it will injure the farm labourer; we think it will enlarge the market for his labour, and give him an opportunity of finding employment, not only on the soil by the improvements which agriculturists must adopt, but that there will also be a general rise in wages from the increased demand for employment in the neighbouring towns, which will give young peasants an opportunity of choosing between the labour of the field and that of the towns. We do not expect that it will injure the landowner, provided he looks merely to his pecuniary interest in the matter[2]." Cobden could not be expected to foresee the changes in the facilities for communication with the Great West which have falsified his confident prediction. It is at all events clear that he would have regarded the serious diminution of the area under cultivation, and of the scope for employment in rural districts, as a very real evil of which account should be taken in attempting to assess the gain and the loss which have come to the country during the era of Free Trade. Cobden

[1] March 12th, 1844.—*Speeches*, vol. I. p. 141.
[2] July 3rd, 1844.—*Ibid.*, vol. I. p. 203. Also February 27th, 1846.—*Ibid.*, p. 382; see p. 64 above.

was not content to consider on what terms goods could be purchased by consumers; just as Tariff Reformers now do, he took the employment of labour and the cultivation of land to be the real proof that good use is being made of national resources.

II.

1. While there is much in Cobden's standpoint and habitual line of argument with which we can heartily agree, it is clear that there were some curious limitations in his political outlook. These were to some extent due to the circumstances of his times, and especially to the current, but mistaken optimism which found full expression in the writings of Cobden's friend, Bastiat. The economists of the day were inclined to assume that if the private interests of individuals were allowed to have free play, the greatest good of the community would be sure to come about mechanically. Monopoly of every kind and exclusive privileges Cobden regarded as injurious; but, where every interest had free play, he had no fear that the pursuit of private gain would be in any way inconsistent with the well-being of the community as a whole. From this point of view, it was only through the advantage which accrued to individuals that the aggregate of interests which made up the national prosperity would be really advanced. He had, as a consequence, no scruple in linking his own personal gain with the success of the cause he had at heart. He was convinced that the repeal of the Corn

Laws would be for the public good, and he prudently endeavoured to enjoy a share in the gain that he anticipated. He speculated, at the time of the Corn Law agitation, for a rise in the value of building land in Manchester, as an incidental effect of the success of his campaign[1]. His confidence in the necessary harmony of general and individual interests was so great that he exhibited a good deal of irritation at his opponents, since he regarded them as short-sighted people whose obstinacy was really injurious to themselves as well as to everyone else. We gather from his speeches that the landlords angered him, not merely because they were selfish, but even more because he regarded them as fools. We can see now that they were not so wholly blind as he supposed; and hence we find it hard to excuse the vein of bitterness which runs through many of his speeches, and the stirring up of class antagonisms to which he lent himself.

He was also inclined to overrate the influence exercised by the material interests of individuals in determining public action, and especially in bringing about changes in international relations. He believed that the demands of foreign consumers for English manufactures would suffice to inaugurate an era of unfettered commercial intercourse and universal peace, almost automatically. This was the ground for his celebrated prophecy—that the whole world would adopt Free Trade if England set the example. In 1846, twelve days before Sir Robert Peel introduced

[1] Morley's *Life of Cobden*, vol. I. p. 159.

his Bill, and when the course he would adopt was still regarded as uncertain, Cobden stated that five years would suffice to bring about this conversion[1]. He thought that the interests of those who used articles of British manufacture would control the policy of foreign countries. He believed that if only Free Trade were once introduced by England a network of harmonious relations would be formed between the various nations of the world, and universal peace would follow, mechanically. But this expectation that the mutual dependence of nations would in itself bring about universal peace has proved to be an idle dream; conscious efforts and mutual concessions are needed to put international relations on a sound and friendly footing; the work that has been done by Lord Lansdowne could never have been accomplished by the methods on which Cobden laid so much stress.

The supposed harmony between duty and interest, which was the basis of Cobden's optimism, is farther exemplified in the view he took of the influence which England might exercise on the other nations of the world. Mr Morley thus summarises his opinions: " England is to-day so situated in every particular of her domestic and foreign circumstances, that by leaving other Governments to settle their own business and fight out their own quarrels, and by attending to the vast and difficult affairs of her own enormous realm and the condition of her people, she will not

[1] 15th January, 1846.—*Speeches*, vol. i. p. 360. See p. 60 above.

only be setting the world an example of noble morality, which no other nation is so happily free to set, but she will be following the very course which the maintenance of her greatness most imperatively commands. It is precisely because Great Britain is so strong in resources, in courage, in institutions, in geographical position, that she can before all other powers afford to be moral, and to set the example of a great nation walking in the paths of justice and peace[1]." We may notice by the way that the extent to which one nation is likely to imitate the example of another may be easily exaggerated. Nations, like individuals, are repelled rather than attracted by anyone who deliberately and gratuitously assumes the position of a model. England has posed as a Free Trade country for half a century, and for the last three decades there have been few indications of any tendency to copy us in this respect. The world at large had noted, under the guidance of Frederic List, that English interests had led to the adoption of Free Trade, and declined to admire this country as an exponent of international morality. Other nations are content to pursue their own interests, so far as they can judge of them, and they are quite clear that our present method of dealing with English interests is not one which they desire to copy.

While Cobden was inclined to idealise any course which was favourable to individual material interests, he was equally ready to condemn any political development to which no such effect could be ascribed,

[1] Morley's *Life of Cobden*, vol. I. p. 95.

since it was likely to take place at the cost of individuals. To him, as to other manufacturers, it appeared a matter of perfect indifference whether our goods were sold to foreigners, or to our countrymen across the sea; so long as Manchester men carried on a profitable trade, they took no account of the question, whether our population and capital were developing the resources of our own Empire, or of some power that might prove to be an antagonist. It was to his mind a distinct advantage that Free Trade, by putting all trading countries on the same footing, would do away with Colonial preferences of every kind; he had no doubt that breaking the ties of interest would increase the difficulties of holding these large and scattered areas together under the authority of the Crown. "The Colonial system," he said, "with all its dazzling appeals to the passions of the people, can never be got rid of except by the indirect process of Free Trade, which will gradually and imperceptibly loose the bands which unite our Colonies to us by a mistaken notion of self-interest[1]." We may leave it to modern Cobdenites to explain whether they have abandoned Cobden's view as to the probable effects of Free Trade, or whether they have a sneaking sympathy with his enthusiasm for lessening the responsibilities and diminishing the prestige of England.

It is a pity that we should be forced to dwell, even in passing, on the faults and limitations of the

---

[1] Letters to H. Ashworth, April 12th, 1842.—Morley's *Life of Cobden*, vol. I. p. 230.

man we commemorate to-day, but our opponents will not allow us to forget them. Those who claim to be his followers are degenerate disciples; for while they copy his mannerisms and reiterate his mistakes, they show no signs of the practical sagacity and ability to learn by experience which rendered him a power in the land.

2. When we take account of the circumstances in which Cobden's great agitation was carried on, we may feel that it is not seriously to his discredit that he should have been guilty of some incidental blunders. In his case they were errors of judgment which any reasonable man might easily make with the information he had before him. Thirty years after the Corn Law of 1815 was passed, it was not unnatural for him to regard the landlords as a body of monopolists who were piling up wealth and power at the expense of the rest of the community. Considering the losses which this class has sustained during the last thirty years, there is no such excuse for the orators who re-echo his denunciations to-day. The landlords have, at all events, been shorn of the exclusive political power which Cobden held to be a public danger.

In 1846 there was much to be said in favour of the view that Free Trade would soon be adopted by all the commercial countries of the world if England would only set the example. Liberalism was in the air, and Sir Robert Peel, in introducing his resolution for the repeal of the Corn Laws, called attention to many signs which seemed to show that such different

countries as the United States, Naples, Norway,
Sweden, Austria and Hanover, might be expected
to take this course.   Cobden's prediction was reasonable enough in 1846 ; but there is no ground for
making a similar forecast to-day, or for alleging that
other countries will follow our lead.   They have
made up their minds to take an opposite course ; it is
merely foolish to suppose that by pursuing our own
line of commercial policy we shall bring other countries round to our views.   Cobden argued for the
repeal of the Corn Laws because he believed it would
be a step to Universal Free Intercourse, and it is idle
to adduce his authority in support of persistence in
the policy of one-sided Free Trade.

Circumstances have changed in another way, since
the time of Cobden ; he mistook the reason for the
origin of the rival industries which were springing up,
and underrated their vitality.   In his day England
towered so far above other countries in industrial
superiority that she could apparently afford to be careless; a policy of *laissez-faire* was good enough.   There
was no obvious need to trouble about privileges and
preferences, for we seemed able to hold our own for
certain in any market in which we got a footing.
During the last fifty years, the development of
manufactures in America and Germany has led to
an international competition in industry, and England
has lost her leading position.   The struggle is now
so keen that we are bound to attend to our manufacturing and commercial interests ; we cannot afford
to let things drift.   There is a double danger in

continuing to pursue the Cobdenite policy to-day.
As our goods are gradually driven from one market
after another, we have diminished opportunities of
purchasing the food we require for our population ;
while the reckless optimism, which *laissez-faire* politicians exhibit in the face of serious dangers, is fatal
to British influence in our Colonies or on our neighbours.   We cannot retain the respect of any other
people if we are too careless, or too arrogant, as a
nation to attend to our own business interests.   Our
insular economic science is content to analyse the
causes of the relative decline of our staple industries,
but is helpless to offer any suggestion as to means by
which England may even maintain her position in the
future.   Nothing can disturb the self-complacent
equanimity of the degenerate disciples of Cobden,
or shake their trust in the efficacy of "the mere
utterance of some formula of economic incantation[1]."

III.

Imperialists in the present day may well claim to
have a share in commemorating the birth of Richard
Cobden.   We have no desire to set him up as a
model to be slavishly copied, for we see that he was
in many ways mistaken.   We would fain bury the
recollection of these errors; but we cannot forget
that, despite his limitations, he did succeed in
awakening Englishmen generally to a sense of their
political privileges, and that he thus made possible

[1] Morley's *Life of Cobden*, vol. ii. p. 343.

the keener life and wider enthusiasms of the present time. Imperialists may draw inspiration from his example, and strive to face the problems of our day with something of the enthusiasm and perspicacity and vigour which he exhibited.

Cobden had a very deep love of his country and pride in her achievements, though he rarely showed it. During his visit to America, however, in 1835, the talk to which he listened fired his British blood, and he gave his thoughts expression in the contrast he drew between England and the United States. "If, many ages hence, your descendants shall be able only to say of their country as much as I am entitled to say of mine now, that for seven hundred years we have existed as a nation constantly advancing in liberty, wealth and refinement, holding out the lights of philosophy and true religion to all the world, presenting mankind with the greatest of human institutions in the trial by jury; and that we are the only modern people that for so long a time withstood the attacks of enemies so heroically that a foreign foe never put a foot in our Capital except as a prisoner (this last is a poser)[1]; if many centuries hence your descendants will be entitled to say something equivalent to this, then, and not till then, you will be entitled to that crown of fame which the historian of centuries is entitled to award[2]." Cobden was patriotic as well as democratic, and we are patriotic

---

[1] He referred to the success of the British arms at Washington in 1813.

[2] Morley's *Life of Cobden*, vol. I. p. 34.

in a larger sense—compatriots with the English
nations beyond the seas. When we remember the
progress which has been made in the diffusion of the
power of self-government both at home and in the
Colonies, and in the improvement of civil administration in our great dependency, we may well be
enthusiastic over the vigorous political life, which
shows itself in the British Empire to-day. Our
Imperialism may have all the characteristics of his
patriotism. " It was not from the side of emotional
sympathy that Cobden started, but from that positive
and scientific feeling for order and good government
which is the statesman's true motive and deepest
passion[1]." We, too, desire to see good government
and order of every kind—including economic order—
throughout the Empire.

We may thus claim to be carrying on the work
which Cobden had at heart, though in some respects
the task that lies before us is harder than that which
Cobden undertook, or at all events than he thought
it was. He believed, mistakenly but still really, that
the changes which he struggled for could be carried
through without cost to anyone. We are under no
such delusion as to the harmony of all the private
interests in a nation, or the complete reconciliation
of private gain with public spirit. There is need,
not to appeal to sordid interests, but to rouse
Englishmen to act on a higher sense of the duty and
destiny of the English race; and this effort is sure to
involve some cost, at least temporarily. The political

[1] Morley's *Life of Cobden*, vol. i. p. 99.

and economic objects we have in view are, as we
believe, worth considerable sacrifice in the hope of
attaining them. Men must learn to look less at
their immediate interests and to think more of the
ultimate results. The narrowest economic prudence
requires that we should pay such a premium now, as
will help to secure our hold on markets where we can
buy provisions and sell our goods, and thus ensure
our national prosperity for a distant future.

Under changed circumstances the means we recommend must be different from those which Cobden
advocated, even though the end in view is much the
same. He set himself to enlarge the circle of exchange, and to remove the fetters which hampered
English trade, and that is our object too. The
obstacles which he desired to remove were self-
imposed; while we want, as free-born Englishmen,
to get rid of the restrictions forced upon us by other
nations. In order to free Englishmen from the
disadvantages under which their trade is now carried
on, it is necessary to bring effective influence to bear
on our industrial rivals, and this can only be done by
a Government that is not only free to negotiate, but
free to retaliate[1].

---

[1] In this connection it is worth while to call attention to some
sentences in a speech of the late Marquis of Salisbury to the
Associated Chambers of Commerce in London, on 4th March,
1891:—"This matter of commercial tariffs is singularly unfitted
for the exercise of that magic spell of remonstrance and objurgation
of which the people of this country are so fond. The object of a
foreign Power in raising its tariffs is to exclude your commodities,
and when you tell them in reproachful tones that the effect of
their tariff will be to exclude your commodities, the only result is

At all events, we may find ourselves in complete accord with Cobden in regard to the tests by which the prosperity of a country can be most truly gauged. He protested against the notion that a low price of corn is the primary consideration with regard to the welfare of the masses. He showed no inclination to set up cheap food as an idol before which political duty and national responsibility, and even future prosperity, might be legitimately sacrificed. We are adopting the economic aims he had in view when we endeavour to see that labour shall be fully employed, and land properly occupied and worked throughout the British Empire. We do not suppose, as he seems to have done, that this result can be obtained mechanically, without either thought or effort; we believe that care and foresight and energy are called for to make the most of every part of our domain. No single formula will apply to the whole of the area over which the British flag waves. There is need to take full account of the resources, not only of the Mother Country, but of every Colony and Dependency, so as at once to do the best for each member, and also to bring them to co-operate together as harmonious parts of a great commercial Empire.

that they say, 'Thank you, I am very much obliged to you. That is just what I intended.' And they give another turn of the screw to the tariff, in order that the effect may be quite unmistakable and leave you to your reproaches. I therefore hope that whatever other policy may be recommended to Her Majesty's Government by these enlightened Chambers, they will not go back to the somewhat antiquated policy of remonstrance, which will do the very reverse of what they intended."—*Supplement to Chamber of Commerce Journal*, p. 30, 10th March, 1891

BACK TO ADAM SMITH.

THERE has been in recent years a tendency on the part of those who are interested in philosophical speculation to revert to the study of Immanuel Kant. The paradoxes and subtleties of dialectic do not seem to afford any means for wrestling seriously with the problems of life. To many it hardly appears worth while to follow the lead of recent thinkers, however bold and ingenious they may be, but rather to get a fresh starting-point by harking back to the Critical Philosophy to which all subsequent speculation owes so much. We may perhaps discern a parallel movement in economics at the present time. The condition of the science is somewhat disappointing: it seems to have lost the hold on the public mind which it enjoyed half a century ago. However delicate the methods of analysis developed by Jevons and his school may be, there is difficulty in bringing the results of their speculations to bear on the actual conditions of affairs. There seems to be good reason to look back not only to Königsberg but to Kirkcaldy.

It would not be uninstructive to press the parallel farther, and insist on the analogies which may be traced between the political philosophy of Kant and that of Adam Smith. Oncken has shown that, different as the men were, they had much in common, and represented a similar reaction from the dominant thought of their day[1]. It is rather my purpose to try to indicate the attitude of mind which was adopted by Adam Smith in his economic investigations. The fun of a humorist sometimes seems to lie not in the words of his jest so much as in the way he said it; and the importance of Adam Smith for us to-day seems to me to be due not so much to the actual doctrines he enunciated as to the views he exemplified in regard to the precise place of economic study in the circle of Moral and Political Sciences, and as to the manner in which it should be pursued. We may, by going back to Adam Smith, find an example as to the most judicious and fruitful course to adopt in attempting to deal with the affairs of our own time.

In trying thus to get at the standpoint of the man, we must be careful not to concentrate attention exclusively on any one of his writings, but to take them as a whole. This is specially necessary in the case of such a book as the *Wealth of Nations*, since it was designedly composed as part of a system of social science, and is confessedly incomplete. By the publication of the notes taken of Adam Smith's Glasgow lectures about 1763[2], we are enabled to see how his treatment of economics was combined with

[1] A. Oncken, *Adam Smith und I. Kant*, p. 61.

[2] *Lectures on Justice and Police*, edited by E. Cannan.

the discussion of the various branches of political life, while his *Theory of Moral Sentiments* gives us a doctrine of human nature which must be taken into account in reading the *Wealth of Nations*. This ethical work is of special importance; it was the book on which Adam Smith particularly prided himself, and he revised it shortly before his death. There is no reason to believe that Adam Smith was in any way conscious of the alleged incompatibility between different parts of his teaching or failed to regard it as a consistent whole[1]. In trying to get a view of the man's standpoint we are bound to go to all the various writings which have survived, rather than confine ourselves to one.

I.

There are two noticeable features which distinguish the work of Adam Smith from that of some of his contemporaries and successors alike. He had a clear view that in economics he was only dealing with one aspect of national life, and that other aspects must be borne in mind as well; while his method of treating the topics is thoroughly empirical. In both respects he remained true to the tradition of the English writers who had dealt with particular parts of the subject which he isolated and examined as a whole—the wealth of the nation. In both respects his work is markedly distinct from that of the French physiocrats : he did not recognise or

[1] A. Oncken, "Des Adam Smith Problem" in (Berlin) *Z. f. Socialwissenschaft*, 1878.

acknowledge much affinity with them because, though their doctrines were similar, the spirit in which they approached the subject was completely opposed to his own habit of mind.

1. There are throughout the *Wealth of Nations* so many passages which expose in sweeping terms the folly of State interference to foster industry and commerce that the hasty reader is left with the impression that Adam Smith had adopted as his ideal a society in which all such attempts at regulation should be abandoned. But a little closer examination will demonstrate that this is not the case; the apparent overstatement on this point occurs in the earlier editions, and is to a considerable extent corrected by the insertions in the third, when the book was so much enlarged. It is abundantly clear that he really assumed the existence of an authority which should be supreme over all economic affairs, and which should occasionally at least interfere with them.

That he did not regard economic considerations as of primary importance is obvious from his often-quoted remarks about the Navigation Act. He commended it as perhaps the "wisest" piece of commercial legislation which had ever been passed in England, although he saw quite clearly that the Act was not "favourable to foreign commerce or to the growth of that opulence which can arise from it [1]." Since "defence" is in his view "of much more importance than opulence," it necessarily follows

[1] *Wealth of Nations*, ed. by Nicholson, p. 188.

that he approved the continued existence of a political authority which regarded all matters of national opulence as falling within its province. All the discussions as to the conditions of retaliation and so forth would be unmeaning, unless he habitually took for granted that political considerations were supreme, and that circumstances might arise at any moment which would require administrative interference. The very exceptions he adduces serve to prove what was the rule in his mind, and that he had not reconciled himself to the extreme *laissez-faire* standpoint from which all State interference in business affairs is in itself condemned. Among the most instructive passages is one inserted in 1784, in which he enters on the history of the exclusive companies. He had already admitted that it was the part of the legislator to promote commerce in general[1], and he argues that it might be a function of the State to promote some particular undertakings of general utility that would strain the resources of individuals[2]. In his days, joint-stock companies were under a cloud[3]; but he regarded them as an institution by which the State might promote certain useful kinds of business, and in this way he justifies the practice of giving a temporary monopoly for some branches of foreign commerce.

So far as we can put the scattered hints together, he seems to have held that the legislator should make

---

[1] *Wealth of Nations*, p. 302.   [2] *Ibid.*, p. 317.

[3] Cunningham, *Growth of English Industry and Commerce in Modern Times*, pp. 448, 816.

it his rule to allow the greatest liberty to each individual to carry on his business in his own way. The
legislator is to be guided by general principles, and
Adam Smith recommends natural liberty as the
general principle which the wise legislator will adopt.
The "insidious animal" who had no guiding principles,
but was merely "directed by the momentary fluctuations of affairs[1]," was on a lower level altogether,
and Adam Smith passes him by contemptuously, and
dwells by preference on the legislators who had
principles—though mistaken ones. It is thus that
he enters on the discussions of the mercantile and the
agricultural systems. In this sense he commends the
system of natural liberty; it is in this sense, too, that
the subject is discussed by other writers of that period,
and that it is true to say that Pitt adopted the system
recommended in the *Wealth of Nations.* He did not
devise taxation with a mere view to the collection of
revenue in the easiest fashion ; Pitt played the part
of the legislator, and tried to bring principles of
justice to bear, in accordance with which the burden
might be placed on the shoulders of those who were
most able to sustain it. Most instructive of all are
the statements of the principles of poor relief and
suggestions in regard to its administration which
Pitt sketched in the debate on Mr Whitbread's
motion for reviving the regulation of wages by the
justices, and fixing a living wage as a protection to
the poor[2]. It was quite consistent with the principles

[1] *Wealth of Nations,* p. 190.
[2] *Parl. Hist.* vol. xxxii. p. 711, Feb. 12, 1796.

of natural liberty, as he understood them, to try to preserve an order in which the economically weak should be cared for and encouraged by the State. Natural liberty was not set up by Adam Smith as something that enables us to dispense with legislators, or that is to override their judgment, but as the principle to which, if they are wise, they will adhere, so far as circumstances allow.

We often hear folk say that it is desirable to give scope for individual liberty, so long as each person allows equal liberty to others; and something of this sort seems to be Adam Smith's idea of what is natural. It is the part of legislation, in his view, to preserve the natural order. On these grounds he expresses approval of drawbacks, even when they cause a loss of customs or excise, since the " natural balance of industry and distribution of labour, which is always more or less disturbed by such duties, would be more nearly re-established by such a regulation[1]." In a similar way he distinguishes the benefit of colonial trade from the effects of colonial monopoly. He would have a free trade secured by treaty, as more beneficial to the public, though less advantageous to merchants[2]. He constantly inveighs against the huckstering spirit of tradesmen, and complains that the mercantile system lent itself to their selfish aims, since it " deranged more or less " the " natural and most advantageous distribution of stock." Projectors were to be kept from meddling : since they " disturb Nature in the course of her operations in human

[1] *Wealth of Nations*, p. 205.
[2] *Op. cit.*, p. 255.

affairs, and it requires no more than to let her alone, and give her fair play in the pursuit of her ends, that she may establish her own designs[1]." Under the system of natural liberty no one would be encouraged to pursue his calling to the detriment of his neighbours.

The natural order, however, was not to be preserved by insisting that the legislator should be a mere looker-on, and never take any action that affected business interests. Adam Smith has no sympathy with Quesnay's prescription of a regimen of perfect liberty and perfect justice. So far is he from assuming it as something that could be taken for granted, that he argues that "if a nation could not prosper without the enjoyment of perfect liberty and perfect justice, there is not in the world a nation which could ever have prospered[2]." Adam Smith knew that a legislator was needed in the actual world, and that he must be a man of tact. As he writes in his *Theory of Moral Sentiments*—

When the legislator cannot conquer the rooted prejudices of the people by reason and persuasion, he will not attempt to subdue them by force, but will religiously observe what, by Cicero, is justly called the divine maxim of Plato, never to use violence to his country, no more than to his parents. He will accommodate, as well as he can, his public arrangements to the confirmed habits and prejudices of the people, and will remedy, as well as he can, the inconveniences which may flow from the want of those regulations which the people are averse to submit to. When he cannot

[1] Dugald Stewart, *Life of Adam Smith* in *Works*, vol. x. p. 68.
[2] *Wealth of Nations*, p. 280.

establish the right, he will not disdain to ameliorate the wrong; but, like Solon, when he cannot establish the best system of laws, he will endeavour to establish the best that the people can bear[1].

Adam Smith was clear that by the comparison of other polities the condition of a country might be improved. He urges any adviser who wishes to rouse a legislator to public-spirited action, that it is easiest to succeed

if you describe the great system of public police which procures these advantages, if you explain the connections and dependencies of its several parts, their mutual subordination to one another, and their general subserviency to the happiness of the society; if you show how this system might be introduced into his own country, what it is that hinders it from taking place there at present, how those obstructions might be removed and all the several wheels of the machine of government be made to move with more harmony and smoothness, without grating upon one another or mutually retarding one another's motions[2].

His criticism of the mechanical social schemes of his own time show how little he was prepared to adopt the conception of a self-acting economic system.

The man of system is apt to be very wise in his own conceit, and is often so enamoured with the supposed beauty of his own ideal plan of government that he cannot suffer the smallest deviation from any part of it. He goes on to establish it completely and in all its parts, without any regard either to the great interests or the strong prejudices which may oppose it: he seems to imagine that he can arrange the different members of a great society with

---

[1] *Theory of Moral Sentiments*, vol. II. p. 103.
[2] *Ibid.*, vol. I. p. 448.

as much ease as the hand arranges the different pieces upon
the chess-board—he does not consider that the pieces upon
the chess-board have no other principle of motion besides
that which the hand impresses upon them, but that, in the
great chess-board of human society, every single piece has
a principle of motion of its own altogether different from
that which the legislator might choose to impress upon it[1].

He was not at all prepared to treat *laissez-faire*
as supplying a system which could be imposed in
England in disregard of political aims and habitual
sentiments. The mechanism of society, as he conceived it, needs constant readjustment if it is really
to accomplish the desired ends.

2. The constant appeal to experience and history
is another feature which distinguishes Adam Smith's
treatment of the subject. In an interesting and
ingenious passage Mr Buckle[2] gives a different account of his method of procedure, and asserts that
while in the *Theory of Moral Sentiments* Adam Smith
derives everything from sympathy, in the *Wealth of
Nations* he deals exclusively with another side, and
follows out the workings of selfishness in all its rami-
fications; but this is to attribute to Adam Smith the
hypothetical and deductive method which was deliberately adopted by some of his followers. His own
course of procedure is entirely different; he does not
take one motive force and analyse it, or measure it—
he observes the phenomena of society as they have
been and are. He discards the conception of value-
in-use, and examines the varieties of exchange. The

---

[1] *Theory of Moral Sentiments*, vol. II. p. 103.
[2] *History of Civilisation*, vol. II. p. 442.

exchange of wares and services is a process which is
always going on in human society; it has been
subjected to regulation and control; the wisdom
of such regulations or of giving the process free play
can be discussed in the light of actual events.   The
increasing importance which Adam Smith attached to
the empirical study of actual phenomena may be most
easily noted by examining the additions which were
inserted in the third edition.   He drew largely on his
stores of knowledge of economic history in order to
accumulate evidence in support of the positions he
had taken.

II.

There is, however, some excuse for regarding
Adam Smith as a mere exponent of *laissez-faire* in
politics and of the deductive treatment in economics,
because of the position he took in regard to some
particular questions.   He was at times so far carried
away by the matter in hand as to be betrayed into
apparent inconsistency; he does not always seem to
be sufficiently mindful of his own principles.

He brings out the importance of the well-being of
the community as overriding individual interests,
when he writes of the Navigation Act.   Still, the
manner in which he allows himself to write, as if the
home trade of consumption were the best criterion of
national prosperity, is open to exception[1].   There

---

[1] "Dr Smith's System of the *Wealth of Nations*, considered
with regard to England and France, in *Suppression of the French
Nobility*, vindicated."   By T. A., p. 54.

are, in particular, one or two topics which he discusses
on the apparent assumption that the private interests
of individuals were all that need be taken into
account. One such passage is his celebrated digres-
sion on the Corn Bounty Law. He looks at the
whole matter from the point of view of cheapness to
the consumer; he thinks he has sufficiently condemned
the Act of 1689 when he shows that it cost the
country the whole amount of the bounty, and that it
did not stimulate agriculture to such an extent as to
lower the price of corn. But there are all sorts of
common interests to be taken into account besides
cheapness: it is a benefit to ensure stability in the
price of the necessaries of life, and this the Act of
1689 helped to do, till it was amended in 1773.
There are political advantages in developing a native
food-supply, and the stimulating of agriculture may
be desirable for the sake of maintaining an effective
and well-nourished population. When we remember
how much the authorities were concerned with the
maintenance of tillage in the later middle ages, how
careful the Tudors and Stuarts were to repress absenteeism in the interests of efficient local government,
and how much there is to be said for utilising the
national capital sunk in the land, we shall see that
Adam Smith was taking a somewhat narrow view in
treating this matter as if it were merely a question of
cheapness, and that the opinions of such men as
Charles Smith and Sir John Sinclair had much in
their favour.

There is also a point in regard to which Adam

Smith was severely taken to task by one of the most eminent economists among his contemporaries, for discarding the empirical method he usually pursued. The view he expressed about apprenticeship was, according to Playfair, determined by his strong prejudice against corporations and regulations of every kind in trade. It served to show " how far prejudice and an opinion once adopted will lead men of the first judgment and genius astray, for it is not to be supposed that any person will stand forward of himself to maintain an opinion against which experience speaks so decidedly[1]." It certainly seems that at the time when the legal obligation for apprenticeship was abolished, Parliament was guided not so much by actual evidence as by mere doctrinaire opinion[2].

III.

While Adam Smith was not always faithful to his own method, his disciples seem to me to have gradually moved away altogether from the standpoint which he endeavoured to take. The temptation to do so was strong. For purposes of economic investigation it is convenient to isolate the subject of wealth, and treat it apart from other social and political phenomena ; and for this purpose we naturally assume that there is no State interference to be taken into account, but that we may follow out what tends to happen on the

[1] W. Playfair: *Inquiry into the Permanent Causes of the Decline of Great and Powerful Nations*, p. 222.

[2] Cunningham: "Economists as Mischief Makers," in the *Economic Review*, vol. IV. p. 10.

supposition of free play for the individual to carry on his work as he chooses. It is easy to pass from taking the principle of *laissez-faire* as an assumption for purposes of investigation, and to elevate it into a maxim for practical guidance. In the early part of the nineteenth century there was a special temptation to make this transition. The evils of State intervention were obvious in many ways: not only were there the mischiefs which Adam Smith had exposed in connection with commerce, but there was much legislation for industry that was out of date, and would have hampered the introduction of machinery and the progress of the industrial revolution. The doctrine of Quesnay and the French economists, which Adam Smith had viewed with suspicion, was attractive to other minds on account of its very simplicity; and the desirability of discarding State interference of any and every kind became a fundamental article of economic faith.

A somewhat similar change took place in the study of individual action. In isolating wealth from other phenomena it was convenient to take the desire of wealth as the dominant motive and, for purposes of investigation, to trace out its working in all directions. This is the hypothetical and deductive method which Buckle extols: it differs from that of other sciences inasmuch as the principle which is applied is merely obtained by introspection and analysis, and is not the result of any serious attempt at induction ; the inductions of Economic Science are, for the most part, curious examples of hasty generalisation from a few isolated particulars[1]. It is easy to argue that the greatest energy of each in pursuing his own interest leads to the greatest aggregate of wealth in the community, and to pass from treating the assumption of self-interest as a convenient hypothesis, to asserting it as a maxim of expediency. Bastiat's doctrine of the harmony of interests rendered the transition plausible, and the result was seen in the clear-cut but one-sided treatment of economic life which characterises the Manchester school.

In the 'Seventies, as I look back on them, the unsatisfactoriness and one-sidedness of such treatment were becoming obvious, and there was another development, but one that takes us still farther away from the position of Adam Smith. It was clear that if social science was to be in any sense complete, other motives than the mere desire of wealth must obtain recognition. An attempt has been made to deal with the complex forces which are at work, by analysing their play in the individual mind. The measurement of motives thus becomes the main business of the economist, and the degrees of utility and dis-utility, to some assumed type of individual, offer the chief field of study. In this way the one-sidedness of the Manchester school is avoided, but the complex order which is studied is not the actual complexity of everyday life, with the higgling of the market; it is merely the imagined process of the individual mind that is analysed. The fundamental

[1] The induction on which Malthus based his law is an important exception.

conception of the science has been surreptitiously and perhaps unconsciously changed. Value-in-Exchange assumes the existence of two bargainers; it gives us a basis for examining their relations. Value-in-Use has to do with the individual and his estimate of utility and dis-utility; we can derive no help from it in co-ordinating observed fact—it is all in a different plane. We cannot but regard it as a grave misfortune that Jevons and his school should have spent their energies so much in analysing the phenomena of value-in-use, which the author of the *Wealth of Nations* had rightly discarded. The ingenious fabric of reasoning that has been built up is curiously alien to Adam Smith's habit of mind. Had some economic expert, who was before his time, expounded to him the mysteries of Consumers' Rent, I think Adam Smith would have been puzzled, as we all have been, to know who paid it, and who gave the receipt; and when he learned that the term had no reference to any transaction that ever had occurred in place or time, I think he would have shown that he took little account of such mental gymnastics.

IV.

It has been left for more recent times to show us a still more startling departure from the standpoint of Adam Smith. Economics became first a hypothetical science, then a subjective science, discussing the play of motives; and now it is fast sinking to the level of a party science. According to Adam Smith's

view it might be possible to lay down general principles which legislators of either party could adopt:
this had been done to a considerable extent in earlier
days by Mun and other exponents of the mercantile
system, and I have endeavoured to show elsewhere
that the system of natural liberty which Adam Smith
commended to the legislator combined the aims of
Whigs and Tories in a most remarkable way[1]. But
just because the idea of preserving the natural order
among conflicting interests has been lost sight of,
economists have been more and more tempted to
constitute themselves the advocates of one powerful
interest or another. This tendency has been particularly obvious in America, where the academic
freedom of economic professors has been seriously
imperilled; and where, on such questions as the
gold standard, or trusts, the professor is expected to
be an advocate who can produce arguments to support
the side that is taken by the patrons of his university.
In the United Kingdom we have been, on the whole,
remarkably free from this abuse; it seems doubtful,
however, whether we shall be able to preserve this
immunity if a precedent which was recently set is
followed in the future. The time which was lately
chosen for organising an expression of expert opinion
on the advantages of Free Trade[2] was surely unfortunate. Whatever may have been the object of that
manifesto, it seems to have been taken by the public

[1] Cunningham, *Growth of English Industry and Commerce in
Modern Times*, p. 597.

[2] The *Times*, 15th August, 1903.

to mean that in the view of several eminent men, Economic Science had spoken with such authority in favour of the policy of Free Imports that any fresh investigation was quite unnecessary. It seemed gratuitous thus to commit the science by anticipation to one special conclusion at the very outset of a political debate in which so much party feeling has been aroused.

It may be a matter of regret that the question as to the fiscal policy of the country should have come to be treated as a matter of party politics, but statesmen who are at a loss for a rallying cry cannot afford to be very scrupulous in choosing their methods of attack. When doubts were first raised, in my recollection, as to the soundness of our industrial prosperity, the discussion had no party character. I remember that in 1877, when I was a University Extension Lecturer in Liverpool, Mr William Rathbone, a well-known Liberal, called attention to the increasing excess of imports in our trade, and argued that there were signs that we were living on our capital. The leading Liberal paper in Liverpool readily acquiesced in his statement of the case. The *Daily Post*[1] wrote as follows :—

We have not, as some Englishmen seem to think it a part of patriotism to believe, an inalienable patent of commercial or manufacturing superiority attaching to England. Other countries produce coal and iron almost as cheaply, perhaps quite as well as we do. In regard to these staples of trade, our margin of preference is small and daily growing less. Germany is better educated,

[1] Jan. 10, 1877.

France is infinitely more thrifty, Belgium, though much given to the invocation of various saints, does not greatly reverence Saint Monday. The Suez Canal is turning trade into its old channel—a channel not favourable to us. All depends upon our power of executing work cheaply and well; of finding out and developing new inventions; of carrying manufacturing industry to the greatest pitch of perfection, and keeping it there. But this we cannot do so long as we are spending much more than we earn, and spending it too in the least profitable way. Mr Rathbone thinks that we have saved ourselves now from a great financial crisis by a large sacrifice of capital, especially of capital which was locked up in foreign securities and has been released at a considerable loss. But this cannot go on for ever. Every crisis which we escape at such a price leaves us poorer and weaker to meet the next.

Nobody seems to have supposed in those days that to raise doubts as to the stability of our industrial system and to commence inquiring into it involved either economic heresy or disloyalty to the Liberal party.

There is a close affinity between the individualism which is assumed by deductive economics and the individualism which is embodied in the political principles of Whigs and Liberals; but there have been occasional breaches. Some twenty years ago it was rather the fashion with Mr Gladstone and his followers to deride the laws of political economy— as inapplicable to Ireland. About the same time Mr Morley was writing the *Life of Cobden*, and he took occasion to disparage the purists who had advocated Insular Free Trade and condemned the policy of commercial treaties.

Nothing can be more unstatesmanlike than to deny that the treaties since 1860 have helped forward the great process of liberating the exchange of the products of their industry among the nations of the world. It is amazing to find able men so overmastered by a mistaken conception of what it is that economic generalisation can do for us, as to believe that they nullify the substantial service thus rendered by commercial treaties of Cobden's type to the beneficent end of international co-operation, by the mere utterance of some formula of economic incantation. If the practical effect of the commercial treaties after 1860, as conceived and inspired by Cobden, has been, without any drawback worth considering, to lead Europe by a considerable stride towards the end proposed by the partisans of Free Trade, then it is absurd to quarrel with the treaties because they do not sound in tune with the verbal jingle of an abstract dogma. It is beside the mark to meet the advantages gained by the international action of commercial treaties, by the formula, "Take care of your imports, and the exports will take care of themselves." The decisive consideration is that we can only procure imports from other countries on the cheapest possible terms on condition that producers in those countries are able to receive our exports on the cheapest possible terms. Foreign producers can only do this on condition that their governments can be induced to lower hostile tariffs; and foreign governments are only able, or choose to believe that they are only able, to lower tariffs in face of the strength of the protected interests, by means of a commercial treaty[1].

It was on these grounds that Mr Morley formerly dissented from the thoroughgoing adoption of the principles of one-sided Free Trade. But times have changed since then. The Opposition has now fallen

[1] Morley, *Life of Cobden*, vol. II. p. 342.

back on abstract Economic Science as if it were an
infallible guide, and the signatories of the manifesto
have compiled ingenious argument, with the apparent
object of giving their support to party tactics. We
have indeed moved a long way from Adam Smith.

V.

The phrase "back to Adam Smith" may have
served to indicate the main point on which I wish to
insist, that economists in the present day would do
well to take the standpoint of the author of the
Wealth of Nations and to adopt his attitude of
mind in carrying on their own investigations. He
looked on Political Economy as a science which laid
down principles for the guidance of the legislator.
He assumes that a man can manage his affairs, and
that Man is master of the conditions which subserve
his well-being. He distinctly dissociated himself from
the view that Man is to be considered "as the materials
of a sort of political mechanics[1]," still less did he
hold that "things are in the saddle and ride mankind." Economics, as a science, helps us to understand the conditions on which prosperity depends;
economics, as an art, gives Man guidance in exercising
his dominion over nature. It is not a mere description
of the play of mechanical forces which shows how
affairs manage themselves.

We are in no danger of supposing that we can go
back to Adam Smith in the sense of imagining that he

---

[1] D. Stewart, *Life* in *Works*, vol. x. p. 68.

has said the last word on any topic, and that there
has been no progress since his time. There has been
an extraordinary development of economic life—a
veritable industrial revolution, reacting on rural
affairs so as to produce an agricultural revolution,
and on the facilities for traffic so as to revolutionise the
system of transport. The phenomena we find presented to us for study are strikingly different from
those he examined. There has been progress, too,
in the facilities for dealing with them ; the collection
of accurate statements of fact has gone on apace, and
the results of careful observation are found in masses
of statistics, and in such forms as are provided by
index numbers. The discussions of four generations
have given us clearer ideas and more precise language
in which to express them. The analysis of the elements
in the process of production enables us to state the
distinctions on which Adam Smith insisted with
greater precision, and at the same time to avoid the
contrast between productive and unproductive classes
in the community, the misleading character of which
was so well exposed by Simon Gray[1]. There have
been other gains as well : the habit of temporarily
isolating one topic—that of wealth—and following
out deductively what will happen when self-interest
has free play, does not give us a law to which human
action conforms ; but it does give us clearly stated
hypotheses which we may apply to the actual facts of
life, with the view of seeing how far the principle has
held true, for any definite place and during any

[1] *All Classes Productive.*

particular period of time. The doctrine of the wage fund is not a universal truth, but it was a very close approximation to the facts of industrial remuneration among operatives in England during the 'Twenties and 'Thirties. The pursuit of Economic Science, as hypothetical and as subjective, has been one-sided and formal, but it has not been useless, since it has served to supply us with better instruments of investigation and better means of stating our results. The value of deductive economics is shown, not by enabling us to dispense with empirical investigation, but by affording us additional help for pursuing it with definiteness and accuracy. This at least is certain: the controversy which is absorbing attention at present has arisen in regard to the conditions of our actual life, and the experience of the last half century. There is little prospect that the public will give serious attention respecting it to the opinion of authorities who are not prepared to approach the fiscal question in the spirit which actuated Adam Smith.

Printed in the United States
By Bookmasters